I0820194

Stitching Together HISTORY

250 Quilts Commemorating the Commonwealth of Virginia

The Virginia Quilt Museum
with Mary W. Kerr and Donna Marcinkowski DeSoto

4880 Lower Valley Road • Atglen, PA 19310

Other Schiffer Books by the Authors:

Southern Quilts: Celebrating Traditions, History, and Designs, Mary W. Kerr, ISBN 978-0-7643-5502-8

Twisted: Modern Quilts with a Vintage Twist, Mary W. Kerr, ISBN 978-0-7643-5170-9

Inspired by the National Parks: Their Landscapes and Wildlife in Fabric Perspectives, Donna Marcinkowski DeSoto, ISBN 978-0-7643-5119-8

Other Schiffer Books on Related Subjects:

Quilts of Virginia, 1607–1899: The Birth of America Through the Eye of a Needle, Virginia Consortium of Quilters' Documentation Project, ISBN 978-0-7643-2465-9

Unconventional & Unexpected, 2nd Edition: American Quilts Below the Radar, 1950–2000, Roderick Kiracofe, ISBN 978-0-7643-6302-3

Inspired by the Nation's Capital: A Fiber Art Souvenir of Washington, DC, Donna Marcinkowski DeSoto, foreword by John Kelly, ISBN 978-0-7643-6324-5

Copyright © 2026 by Mary W. Kerr and Donna Marcinkowski DeSoto

Library of Congress Control Number: 2025940005

The statements and opinions included in the quilts' descriptive texts have been provided by the artists and edited for clarity. They do not represent the opinions of the authors and do not constitute an endorsement of the opinions of the authors or publisher.

All rights reserved. No part of this work may be reproduced or used in any form or by any means—graphic, electronic, or mechanical, including photocopying or information storage and retrieval systems—without written permission from the publisher.

The scanning, uploading, and distribution of this book or any part thereof via the Internet or any other means without the permission of the publisher is illegal and punishable by law. Please purchase only authorized editions and do not participate in or encourage the electronic piracy of copyrighted materials.

"Schiffer," "Schiffer Publishing, Ltd.," and the pen and inkwell logo are registered trademarks of Schiffer Publishing, Ltd.

Designed by Kate North
Cover design by Kate North
Cover art: *Virginia Reelin'* by Lois Born (see page 200)
Type set in P22 Avocet Light Pro/Kigelia LGC/Arno Pro

ISBN: 978-0-7643-7098-4
ePub: 978-1-5073-0639-0
Printed in China

10 9 8 7 6 5 4 3 2 1

Published by Schiffer Publishing, Ltd.
4880 Lower Valley Road
Atglen, PA 19310
Phone: (610) 593-1777; Fax: (610) 593-2002
Email: info@schifferbooks.com
Web: www.schifferbooks.com

For our complete selection of fine books on this and related subjects, please visit our website at www.schifferbooks.com. You may also write for a free catalog.

Schiffer Publishing's titles are available at special discounts for bulk purchases for sales promotions or premiums. Special editions, including personalized covers, corporate imprints, and excerpts, can be created in large quantities for special needs. For more information, contact the publisher.

Dedicated to all quilters past, present, and future whose hearts and creativity inspire us to find our voices in this beloved art form.

Contents

Buhl-Bushong Quilt, New Market, Virginia, 87" × 87", circa 1855.
Collection of the Virginia Quilt Museum.

Foreword

I'm used to studying a quilt to find out its history; the who, what, why, when, and where it was made. Every quilt tells a story, even if it's just "I like this color or pattern or flower" or "I made this for you." That's how I started quilting, making a baby quilt for a friend. There are any number of reasons to make a quilt, and in the case of the quilts in this collection, the reason is to tell the viewer something about Virginia. Quilters use their needles not just to sew fabric but to tell a story. They have long been the folk-art historians of their day, capturing in cloth the important events and people of our nation's history. A quilt can be a material record of the life, beliefs, history, and inspirations of the maker. This is true of the treasured antique quilts preserved at the Virginia Quilt Museum and just as true of the new quilts shared in this book.

As the commonwealth of Virginia celebrates its 250th anniversary, we find an opportunity to reflect on the evolution of Virginia and the spirit of a state that has helped shape the nation. It's a time to celebrate not just the historical events but also the cultural contributions of its people through the centuries. And what better medium to do this than quilts.

The Virginia Quilt Museum has used the occasion of the semiquincentennial to call on quilters to tell the stories of this history through representations that fit into four themes: "Power of Place," "Unfinished Revolutions," "Virginia Experiments," and "We the People." From the earliest Indigenous tribes to the waves of settlers who arrived seeking freedom and opportunity, to the enslaved Africans whose labor built much of the state's economy, and to the many voices of today that represent the rich diversity of the commonwealth—Virginia's history is itself a quilt stitched of many threads.

The past four hundred years of life in Virginia provides much material for storytelling. Just the list of descriptive identities is revealing; it was the settlement at Jamestown in 1607, then named Virginia for Elizabeth, the Virgin Queen, then and now called the "Old Dominion," and includes several maternal titles: the "Mother of a Nation," the "Mother of Presidents," and the "Mother of States." There's much to share about the landscape also. The panorama includes 500 miles of coastline hugging the Atlantic Ocean, lush valleys, rolling mountains, peaceful rivers, majestic waterfalls, deep caverns, and caves.

Attributed to Thomas Jefferson is the saying "On the whole, I find nothing anywhere else . . . which Virginia need envy."

Much of this you will find depicted and interpreted in the collection of 250 quilts that follow. Here, contemporary quilters, me included, have shared something from the events or people or land that resonated with them and motivated them to render it in fabric. Some found inspiration in the rich history, some in the struggles, some in the flora and fauna, or some, as in my case, in some fact previously unknown to me. These quilters have been inspired by the complexities of Virginia, capturing its natural beauty, its historical landmarks, its people, and its ongoing progress. You will see historic figures such as the presidents you easily recognize, but also individuals who are less well known but have nevertheless had an impact. These quilts include monuments that we all know, but also places of quiet beauty in the landscape. Virginia's long quilting history is addressed with several patterns attributed to or named for Virginia; the nineteenth-century quilt patterns like Virginia Reel and Virginia Star are now traditional patterns that quilters everywhere use. And in this book, quilters continue the tradition of using their needles to tell their stories through their quilts.

Anniversaries provide an opportunity to reflect on the rich past, the current efforts, and the future possibilities. In celebrating Virginia's 250th anniversary, we not only honor its storied past but also recognize the creative forces that continue to define its identity. May this collection serve as a reflection of the heart and soul of Virginia—its beauty, its complexity, and its boundless potential. As we look back on the remarkable journey of the past 250 years, let us also look forward with hope and anticipation to the future and the many quilts yet to be made.

Welcome to Virginia through the eyes of its quilters.

Bunnie Jordan
Quilt historian and former Virginia Quilt Museum board member

Maple Leaf, Harrisonburg, Virginia, 92" × 99", circa 1840. Collection of the Virginia Quilt Museum.

Preface

In early 2022, I began considering how the Virginia Quilt Museum (VQM) could participate in America's Semiquincentennial. That March, I attended the Virginia Association of Museums conference in Richmond, and the 250th was a popular topic of conversation. I struggled to think of a way the VQM could be included in this commemoration. VQM has over three hundred quilts in our permanent collection, but the oldest dates to 1806—a full thirty years after the signing of the Declaration of Independence. This meant we couldn't pull together an exhibition from our collection.

In May 2023, I was inspired by Kelly Zuber, a representative from the Virginia Consortium of Quilters. She shared that her guild in Roanoke had recently celebrated their fortieth anniversary. The guild had created an exhibition of forty art quilts for their anniversary, with a quilt representing each year of their existence. I wondered if we could expand that idea and do a larger-scale project focused on the whole of Virginia. What would happen if we created a mini-quilt challenge: 250 quilts for the 250th anniversary, one for each year of Virginia's history as a state?

I sat down and wrote an outline, a timeline, and some thoughts I had about the project. Looking back at that document now, it is surprising to me how much this idea has grown and changed over time but how much it has stayed the same.

I shared it with the executive committee of the VQM Board of Directors. I knew that this would be a huge, multiple-year project and would need to be approved by the board. The executive committee was very receptive and offered feedback and encouragement. I reached out to Donna DeSoto, who was thrilled to hear of this idea and encouraged me to move forward with it.

From there the project quickly took shape, and the museum's full board approved the project in July 2022, and the project evolved into its current form. Instead of a quilt for each year, we decided to be more inclusive, and we put out a request for quilts to commemorate a person, place, event, thing, or idea from Virginia or West Virginia's history. Our call for entries welcomed quilters of varying levels of quilting experience. For uniformity, we asked that each quilt measure a finished 20" by 20" size.

We were honored to receive a grant from the Virginia American Revolution 250 Commission (VA250), and we were able to use that money to promote the project, host webinars on different topics with speakers from other cultural institutions, and pay for the needed technology.

I am thrilled with the quilts in this project. Artists sent us their best work and truly embraced the Stitching Together History concept. The committee selected the 250 quilts included here, and we are honored to share them in print and on exhibit. Thank you to everyone who created a quilt, everyone who helped promote this project, and especially to Donna DeSoto and Mary Kerr for tackling the writing of this book. Donna and Mary guided me through this project, and it would not be the success it is without their involvement.

Alicia Thomas
Executive Director, the Virginia Quilt Museum

Crossed Tulips, unknown maker, Virginia, 86" × 92", dated 1862. Collection of the Virginia Quilt Museum.

CHAPTER 1

Power of Place

The physical boundaries of Virginia have changed many times, and the physical features of all of the United States are constantly changing. From natural erosion wearing down the Appalachian Mountains, to creating artificial lakes, to building roads and canals, to climate-change-related weather events, the physical landscape of Virginia is continuously evolving.

These changes have influenced people and events throughout history. The physical features of an area can have far-reaching effects. Our talented quilters thought about the history of the Eastern Shore and how proximity to the Chesapeake Bay and the Atlantic Ocean shaped that region, how the Great Dismal Swamp affected the movement of early European settlers, and how the mountains of the western part of the state affected migration and the culture of the region.

The quilts shown here commemorate local landmarks, treasured memories of special places, our beautiful countryside, Virgina plants and native creatures, and more.

This *Wheel of Time* quilt was created in 1860 by Wythe County resident Eveline Wampler Poff for her wedding to John David Miller. Her tiny pieces and the circular movement expertly reflect the mountainous beauty and ruggedness of this south-central Virginia county.

Wheel of Time Quilt, Wythe County, Virginia, 82" × 82.5", circa 1860.
Collection of the Virginia Quilt Museum.

MONA B. ALDERSON
Mountain City, Tennessee

Mount Rogers from Elk Garden

This is a view from the town of Elk Garden, West Virginia, looking toward Mount Rogers, the highest mountain in Virginia. The focal point of the Mount Rogers Recreation Area and Grayson Highlands State Park, Mount Rogers is a significant natural landmark and a place of unspoiled beauty located in southwestern Virginia. The mountain's geology and spruce-fir forest are unique, making this a highlight of the Appalachian Trail. The mountain is named for William Barton Rogers, Virginia's first state geologist, who went on to found the Massachusetts Institute of Technology, established in 1861.

NICKI ALLEN

Springfield, Virginia

Blue Ridge Sunrise

The Blue Ridge mountains are known for having a bluish color when viewed from a distance. The color comes from a chemical compound released from the trees. Also shown are the flowering dogwood, which is the state flower as well as the state tree, and the northern cardinal, the state bird, which is recognized by its brilliant color and beautiful calling sound.

ARLENE L. BLACKBURN

Union Hall, Virginia

Piedmont Mill Historic District

Piedmont Mill Historic District (a.k.a. Cummins Mill) is a nineteenth-century gristmill complex in rural Franklin County, Virginia. The 1866 mill building on the banks of Maggodee Creek was essential to the early rural residents. In 1870, it was the most powerful mill in Franklin County and maintained operations until 1963. The district was listed on the National Register of Historic Places in 2009.

NICKI ALLEN
Springfield, Virginia

Corbin Cabin

Corbin Cabin, a restored structure in Shenandoah National Park, represents the many homes that were destroyed in order to create the park. In the 1930s, Shenandoah National Park was pieced together from over three thousand individual tracts of land, necessitating five hundred families to be moved from their homes. The homes were subsequently destroyed by Civilian Conservation Corps volunteers to ensure that no one would return to live there. Throughout the park, one can find isolated chimneys that are remnants of these homesteads. Corbin Cabin represents all those families forced to move out of the mountains that had been their home for generations. Many families did not move willingly, and in some instances, they were physically removed. Only recently have organizations such as the Blue Ridge Heritage Project created memorials to honor the people who were displaced.

NICKI ALLEN
Springfield, Virginia

Majestic Elk

Elk were historically found throughout eastern North America, including Virginia. But by the late 1800s, unsustainable hunting and habitat changes resulted in the extirpation of the eastern elk. The last survivor of Virginia's elk herd was killed in 1855 in Clarke County. Over the next hundred years, several efforts to reintroduce elk to Virginia were attempted but failed. Elk were successfully reestablished between 2012 and 2014, and now there is a thriving herd of more than 250 elk in southwestern Virginia. They are an important part of Virginia's natural history, and their return is a symbolic reminder of efforts to restore species and habitats. They connect modern conservation efforts to Virginia's past.

DIANA ANGLERO
Stephens City, Virginia

Burwell-Morgan Mill

This mill is on the National Register of Historic Places and one of the oldest operational gristmills in the country, located in the heart of the Shenandoah Valley. In 1785, General Daniel Morgan joined efforts with Colonel Nathaniel Burwell to build this waterpowered mill, in an area that would become the village of Millwood. As business flourished, the mill was the center of community life for many years, and it produced more than 300,000 pounds of flour and meal each year. This is a living record of the production of wheat in Clarke County, Virginia, and the northern Shenandoah Valley. The Clarke County Historical Association acquired the remains of the mill in 1964. After restoration, it opened in 1972 as an operating mill-museum. Freshly ground flour, cornmeal, and grits are available for sale at the mill. Each year, during spring and fall, the Burwell-Morgan Mill becomes an extraordinary art gallery.

ANNE AUBRY
Front Royal, Virginia

Indian Burial Mounds of West Virginia

When the first Europeans explored the area now known as West Virginia, they recorded more than four hundred earthen structures, often built in large complexes along major rivers. It has since been determined that the mounds were built by prehistoric Native Americans and were part of what is known as the Woodland period. Most belonged to the Adena culture, which flourished from 200 BCE to 200 CE. Tragically, most of these mounds were excavated by antiquarians or simply destroyed, many of them as recently as the 1960s. Today, only about ten of these structures remain. The best known of these are the Grave Creek Mound in Moundsville, West Virginia, and the Criel Mound in South Charleston, West Virginia.

ANNE AUBRY
Front Royal, Virginia

Yorktown 1781

The siege and battle of Yorktown was the last major land battle of the Revolutionary War. It took place from September 30 to October 19, 1781, in the area around Yorktown and Gloucester Point along the York River. This marked a turn in the war and ended with the surrender of General Cornwallis. The battle is also notable for the engagement of French troops led by General Rochambeau alongside Washington's army. Surrounded on all sides by enemy fire and unable to get reinforcements due to the blockade of the Chesapeake Bay by the French fleet, Cornwallis had no other choice but to surrender. Even though the peace treaty between the British and their former colonies was not signed until 1783, the victory at Yorktown is considered to have precipitated the end of the war in North America and cemented George Washington's reputation as a great commander in chief.

MARY BETH BELLAH
Charlottesville, Virginia

Wilderness Trail

Giles County, Virginia, is home to an area called "Virginia's Mountain Playground." Six popular hiking trails run along the 37 miles of the New River and New River Water Trail that separates Virginia and West Virginia in the southwestern part of our state. These trails provide great wilderness views of Mill Creek, Cascade Falls, and the Appalachian Trail. They provide rewarding adventures both for day trips and long-distance hikes.

VIRGINIA BENNETT
Bristow, Virginia

ELLEN ORANGE
Midland, Virginia

Brentsville Historic Site

The Historic Preservation Division holds a festival each fall at the Historic Brentsville Site, which serves as a gathering place for the community and allows a glimpse of the past to compare with the current growth and lifestyles that will continue to change in the future. These foundations never change: community, faith, education, and justice.

LINDA BILLARD
Fredericksburg, Virginia

Historic Fredericksburg: Preserving Virginia's Built Legacy

This is a timeless river view of Fredericksburg, now and then. History is recorded in these buildings. Each one that is torn down because it is old is another bit of history lost. Fredericksburg's dedication to saving its history through preservation is a model for true urban renewal. John Smith mapped the area in 1608, and the town was chartered in 1728. As a prominent Rappahannock River port, it hosted many Revolutionary War–era figures, including George Washington; his mother, Mary; his sister Betty and her husband, Fielding Lewis; future president James Monroe; and the Marquis de Lafayette. Preservation efforts include the forty-block historic district, on the National Register of Historic Places. It contains 350 eighteenth- and nineteenth-century buildings, including the homes of Mary Washington and Betty Washington Lewis; the old courthouse, the only Virginia building designed by James Renwick; and the Charles Dick House (ca. 1740), the oldest extant building in Fredericksburg.

E. GAIL BILLINGSLEY
Blacksburg, Virginia

KARIN TAUBER
Blacksburg, Virginia

Discovery Inland Journey

In 1607, after the initial landing of three ships carrying 105 passengers and 39 crew members to the Virginia shores, Captain John Smith left Jamestown on the ship *Discovery*. This was the smallest of the ships and was used to explore and map coastal waterways and the Chesapeake Bay, searching for badly needed food. Smith regularly traded with the Powhatan communities but was later captured by warriors from that tribe. He was said to have covered an estimated 3,000 miles.

E. GAIL BILLINGSLEY
Blacksburg, Virginia

KARIN TAUBER
Blacksburg, Virginia

Powhatan Hunting Grounds

A dense forest filled with diverse and abundant wildlife and plants was home to an estimated 14,000 to 21,000 Powhatan people when the English settlers arrived in 1607. The Powhatan were Eastern Woodland Indians, sometimes also referred to as Algonquians. Their tribal lands encompassed all of what is now known as the Virginia Tidewater area. The Native American tribes living in Virginia in the early 1600s settled away from the coast but used these areas for fishing, hunting, and gathering. The rivers and inlets were plentiful with fish. There was a lot of game in the area: raccoon, deer, opossum, turkey, squirrel, and rabbit, among others. The Powhatans' planting, hunting, fishing, and gathering followed the rhythm of the seasons. In 1608 the Powhatans brought food to the dwindling population in Jamestown, likely saving the depleted and sick settlers from perishing.

E. GAIL BILLINGSLEY
Blacksburg, Virginia

KARIN TAUBER
Blacksburg, Virginia

Virginia Bobcat

When settlers arrived on the shores of Virginia, they were taken by the diversity of wildlife, flora, and fauna. This was a rich hunting ground for the Powhatan Indians. The native Virginia bobcat, with its silver hair, long "sideburns," and black streaks, roamed the lush forest. This species is a medium-sized cat that generally weighs between 10 to 20 pounds and has a swift, distinctive bounding gait. Virginia's westernmost counties, Lee and Scott, hold the greatest concentration of bobcats, but they can be found throughout the state in heavily forested, mountainous terrain. They are shy and secretive and avoid populated areas.

DEBRA BINGHAM

Fairfax, Virginia

Virginia Bluebells

Bluebells were found by early colonists in Virginia. They are perennial plants native to Virginia and eastern North America. They bloom every spring for two to three short weeks, usually in April. Bluebells can be found in the shade alongside creeks, streams, and rivers. The lovely sky-blue to pinkish-purple flowers are bell shaped, and two places they are most abundant are at Bull Run and Riverbed Regional Park.

LOIS BORN

Woodstock, Virginia

Shenandoah Barn

Throughout its 250 years of statehood, agriculture in the Shenandoah Valley has supported the commonwealth of Virginia. Barns symbolize family farms that have been the backbone of agriculture in this picturesque valley. Produce from here significantly contributes to the thriving Virginia economy. A barn quilt highlights this melding of our agriculture and quilting traditions.

LINDA BOONE
Ruckersville, Virginia

Seneca Rocks

Seneca Rocks is part of a national recreation area in the Monongahela National Forest. It is an instantly recognizable landmark in West Virginia. Rising nearly 900 feet above the North Fork River, it was captured by sketch artists as early as 1853, when the area still belonged to the Commonwealth of Virginia. Currently a popular spot for recreational climbing, it was used by local World War II soldiers to train for mountain assaults in Italy. Its majesty is inspiring to outdoorsmen and artists alike.

KATHLEEN BRANCH
Hanover, Maryland
DIANA HAMIL
Morgantown, West Virginia

Prospect Valley, Virginia, 1776

This is a portrayal of the landscape in 1776 of Prospect Valley and Robinson Run in Harrison County, Virginia. The history of Prospect Valley includes the movement of Virginians into the western mountains. By the mid-1700s, explorers and settlers were moving west. William Robinson was patented a large tract of land in Harrison County in 1774 and established the community of Prospect Valley. It was one of the first communities in the area, with the first gristmill and sawmill. The development of Prospect Valley coincides with the signing of the Declaration of Independence in 1776, and the settlement and growth of the western side of the Appalachian Mountains after the Revolutionary War. The overlaid map of Virginia and West Virginia shows the two separate states today. The western part of Virginia east of the Appalachian Mountains became a separate state in 1863. The small community thrived into the 1960s, when its land was taken for the coal-powered Harrison County, West Virginia, electricity-generating power plant.

BARBARA BRUMMOND
Forest, Virginia

Dawn of a New Day

Here is a view from a shoreline, looking east, as the sun begins to break over the horizon. For each person who has stood and looked to the dawn, a different story is told: a native concerned for the changes that immigrants are bringing; an explorer or businessman wondering what treasures and resources may be exploited and exported; a settler hoping for a better life in the "New World," perhaps fleeing religious persecution; an enslaved person brought against his will, packed tightly into a cargo hold, enduring a treacherous journey; a soldier following orders from afar; or a revolutionary demanding independence. Then as now, how one interprets a sunrise is a product of his or her background, influenced by past experiences, cultural upbringing, personal beliefs, and overall life story.

BARBARA BRUMMOND
Forest, Virginia

The House Is on Fire

This piece was inspired by the book *The House Is on Fire* by Rachel Beanland, which chronicles the burning of a theater and its tumultuous aftermath in Virginia in 1811. In Richmond on the day after Christmas in 1811, the Richmond Theater was packed, with six hundred in attendance. It was booked as a fundraiser to support the family of a much-loved and recently deceased actress, Elizabeth Poe. She left behind three young children, including two-year-old Edgar Allan Poe. The fast-moving fire resulted in the deaths of seventy-two people; fifty-four were women. The fire captured the public imagination in part because some victims were wealthy and distinguished, including the governor of Virginia. According to historian Meredith Henne Baker, later, even-far-more-deadly fires did not prompt similar memorials or legendary tales of lovers dying in each other's arms. Two hundred years later, however, the fire has been "gradually forgotten . . . , no more than a footnote and a crumbling white memorial that once earned the wonder of a nation." The memorial and a church built over the original site stand today.

BARBARA BRUMMOND
Forest, Virginia

McAfee Knob

McAfee Knob is an amazing geological feature located on Catawba Mountain, at an elevation of 3,197 feet. This is the tallest mountain in the area and 15 miles from Roanoke. It is known as the most photographed point of the Appalachian Trail. The vista offers panoramic views of the Blue Ridge Mountains and Catawba Valley. The knob is named for James McAfee, a Scotch Irish settler who purchased the land in 1740. The beauty and history of this memorable site is important, but the preservation for the future is paramount. The Appalachian Trail Conservancy, the Conservation Fund, and the Roanoke Appalachian Trail Club continue to add more acres of permanently protected land to the area. Acreage has been acquired to help preserve the abundant views from McAfee Knob, to improve access to the trail, and to provide greater conservation of the surrounding area, to ensure enjoyment of McAfee Knob for generations to come.

STEPHANIE BURKE
Marshall, Virginia

Wallops Island

Wallops Island on the Eastern Shore is a beautiful natural area next to Chincoteague and Assateague Islands. It is home to the NASA Wallops Flight Facility, including the Mid-Atlantic Regional Spaceport. Rocket launches support scientific research for NASA, weather research for NOAA, and many other customers. Wallops Island includes a national wildlife refuge that protects a fragile coastal marshland ecosystem and a sea-level fen. The site is an important part of the Eastern Migratory Flyway and provides safe harbor for birds as they travel on seasonal migratory journeys. This island was granted to John Wallop in 1692 by the king of England and was later seized by Virginia for unpaid taxes. Over many years, the island was used for myriad purposes, leading to its current uses. It provides an interesting juxtaposition of both high-tech research and unspoiled natural beauty.

BEVERLY BURROUGHS

Burke, Virginia

My Happy Place

The brook trout was designated as the official fish of Virginia in 1993. In 2011, it was redesignated as the official freshwater fish; the striped bass was named as the official saltwater fish. Brook trout can be found in over four hundred of Virginia's streams and ponds. They eat insect larvae, small fish, and crayfish and are considered to be the most colorful trout native to Virginia. In this piece, this brook trout has found his happy place in a river surrounded by Virginia quilt blocks. Incidentally, the Virginia quilt block shown was chosen to be Virginia's state quilt block by *Hearth and Home* magazine in 1907.

MARY KERR

Woodbridge, Virginia

Shenandoah Spring

Shenandoah National Park is home to a thriving population of black bears, and every spring the cubs come out to play. It is estimated that five hundred to a thousand black bears are living in the park, since it provides large areas of contiguous, high-quality forest habitat. This quilt was created from a tea towel that was painted with Tri-Chem paints in the 1960s. It is bordered with fragments of a hexagon quilt from that same era. It was expertly quilted by Shannon Shirley.

LYN COLEMAN
Moneta, Virginia

Booker T. Washington Birthplace

On a former slave owner's tobacco plantation in Franklin County, Virginia, this national monument park focuses on the injustices of slavery, the impacts of the Civil War, and the Emancipation Proclamation. It also recognizes the significant contributions of Booker T. Washington. Booker was born enslaved in 1856 to his mother, Jane, and an unknown white father, and his early childhood was typical of many enslaved persons who lived in a windowless log cabin with a dirt floor, but he attended what is now Hampton University, in Virginia and, later, Wayland Seminary in Washington, DC. At twenty-five, Booker was appointed as the first leader of what is now the Tuskegee Institute in Alabama. As an adult, he used his skills as an orator and leader to provide educational opportunities for African Americans.

LYN COLEMAN
Moneta, Virginia

Roanoke Star

The Roanoke Star stands high on Mill Mountain in Roanoke and gives the city the nickname of "Star City of the South." Constructed in 1949 by the Kinsey Sign Company, it was initially funded by a merchant association but later was turned over to the city to pay for the electricity cost. While it was intended to be lit only at Christmas, it soon became a tourist attraction and was lit entirely in white every single night, except for patriotic holidays (red, white, and blue) and tragic events (shining solely in red). Its weight is 60,000 pounds, with 2,000 feet of neon tubing, and its height is 88.5 feet, allowing it to be seen from 60 miles away when lit.

LYN COLEMAN
Moneta, Virginia

Save the Wild Turkeys

Early settlers in Virginia relied on wild turkeys for food, but in the early 1900s the wild turkey population dwindled, due to commercial marketing of the meat. In 1912, conservation concerns led to passing the "Robin Bill," which made the sale of wild turkeys in the open market illegal. With the creation of the Virginia Game Department in 1916, the bill was enforced and turkeys were protected. Efforts were made to restore their presence in the abounding natural habitat, and wild turkeys again flourished in Virginia. The Turkey in the Straw traditional quilt block is seen in the background of this piece.

DAWN CONRAD
Victoria, Virginia

Victoria, Virginia

Victoria, Virginia, is a railroad town located in Lunenburg County. Victoria's roundhouse with turntable, water tower, and station house are depicted here along with a 1900s steam locomotive. Near the midway point on the Tidewater Railway, it was founded in 1906 as a new town with ample space for railway offices and shops and was named for Queen Victoria. Victoria's large rail yard included a roundhouse with turntable and coaling and water facilities. It was designed for large steam locomotive maintenance and crew changes. Offices for the Virginia Railroad's Norfolk Division were later built as a second floor above the original station building. The Virginia General Assembly granted a charter and incorporated the town on March 11, 1916. A "small" town built by America's railroad industry, it has survived against all odds after modernization of the transportation of America took place in the early 1950s. Victoria has evolved while holding tightly to her roots and is one of the many beautiful small towns of Virginia still surviving today.

BEVERLY AND BILL DASCH
Manassas, Virginia

Battle of Hampton Roads

This pivotal battle in Virginia history was the first time that two ironclad ships, warships that were covered with iron plates, were in battle with one another. This happened in the early stages of the Civil War, on March 9, 1862. The battle between the USS *Monitor* and the *Merrimack* demonstrated the innovative engineering and tactical capabilities and limitations of using ironclads rather than wooden ships. It sparked the continuing, worldwide development of armored warships, including many still being built today in the area of Hampton Roads. Incidentally, neither side won this particular battle, but it set a whole new stage in naval warfare.

POLLY DAVIS
Warrenton, Virginia

Emancipation Oak

In Hampton, Virginia, there stands a magnificent southern oak, *Quercus virginiana*, known as the Emancipation Oak. Under its stately branches, the first southern public reading of Lincoln's Emancipation Proclamation took place in 1863. Also protected by these branches were lessons in reading and writing that were given by a free Black woman named Mary Smith Kelsey Peake. Since Union soldiers held the nearby Fort Monroe, the fort offered asylum to escaped enslaved persons who were the students of these life-altering lessons.

POLLY DAVIS
Warrenton, Virginia

One of the Barn Crew

The beautiful countryside of Virginia is well known as being horse country. Since 1610, when the first horses arrived with the settlers in the Virginia colonies, this area has had a rich history with horses. Their original purpose as farm labor and transportation has evolved over time. Today nearly a million people travel to Virginia every year to enjoy over 1,200 horse shows, events, races, hunts, and trail rides. The oldest horse show in the country is the town of Upperville's Colt & Horse Show, which started in 1853 and is still celebrated as an annual event on the same grounds.

DONNA DESOTO
Fairfax, Virginia

Back Bay National Wildlife Refuge at Sandbridge

Just a short distance from the hustle and bustle of Virginia Beach are more than 9,200 acres of marsh, beaches, dunes, woodlands, and farm fields. Extensive trails afford numerous opportunities for birdwatching. The refuge provides an important habitat for nearly three hundred recorded species of waterfowl and shorebirds, including numerous threatened species. Much activity occurs during winter and spring migrations. River otters, white-tailed deer, raccoons, bobcats, reptiles, and amphibians abound.

ROBERTA DEWEES
Springfield, Virginia

George Washington Surveyed Here

George Washington is best known as a military man and first president of the United States, but he began his career as a surveyor throughout Virginia. His mother, Mary Ball Washington, while not a surveyor herself, played a significant role in shaping George's career by encouraging his interest in land surveying. She provided him with his father's surveying equipment and hired a tutor to teach him. George later studied with his neighbor, Lord Fairfax. His career began when he surveyed his property at Mount Vernon, and he later worked throughout Virginia. His initials are carved in the rocks in Natural Bridge, placed while he surveyed in that area.

EILEEN DOUGHTY
Vienna, Virginia

The National 9/11 Pentagon Memorial

On the morning of September 11, 2001, hijackers crashed American Airlines Flight 77 into the Pentagon, destroying part of the outer ring of the building. The National 9/11 Pentagon Memorial honors the 184 people killed in that act of terrorism: 125 inside the Pentagon and 59 passengers and crew on the jet. There are many elements to the memorial. What is symbolized in my quilt, with a dashed-pattern fabric, are the individual cantilevered benches oriented along the flight line. The benches are arranged chronologically by age of the associated person. The youngest victim, Dana Falkenberg, was only three. Despite being located near a busy city and only steps away from the gigantic Pentagon, the memorial allows quiet contemplation of a tragic day in US history.

ANNABEL EBERSOLE
Williamsburg, Virginia

The Hearth at William & Mary College

This memorial, a brick-and-stone building, commemorates the enslaved who worked at the College of William & Mary. Dedicated in 2022, *Hearth: Memorial to the Enslaved* is a memorial to the enslaved Americans who built and supported the College of William & Mary over a period of 172 years. The memorial includes first names of enslaved individuals; there are numerous references to "Unknown." Hearth is a powerful tribute to a bleak chapter of American history. The plaque on a nearby wall reads as follows:

"William & Mary enslaved Africans and African Americans for over 172 years. This memorial seeks to remember and honor those individuals through the symbol of the hearth which evokes at once the harsh, forced labor of chattel slavery as well as a place of gathering, strength, and community. Indeed, enslaved people made a way out of no way."

SARAH ENTSMINGER
Ashburn, Virginia

Morven Park

Morven Park in Leesburg, Virginia, was once the home of Virginia governor Westmoreland Davis and his wife, Marguerite. They purchased it in 1903. Managed by the Westmoreland Davis Foundation, the property is open to the public and hosts a wide variety of events, especially equestrian events. The mansion is now a museum, and Mrs. Davis's boxwood gardens continue to be maintained. Carriage Road, once the primary approach for the mansion, is where one can see the magnificent tree that inspired this piece and the reliance, strength, and beauty of age it represents.

SARAH ENTSMINGER
Ashburn, Virginia

Piscataway Crossing

White's Ford was an important passage over the Potomac River during the Civil War. It was named after Captain Elijah White, a Confederate cavalry officer whose farm was on the Virginia side of the ford. In recent years, the area was renamed Piscataway Crossing for the Native American tribe who settled on a 194-acre island in the Potomac River across from the ford. The island provided protection from hostile tribes and offered a buffer against encroaching white settlers. The Piscataway built a palisaded fortress with traditional long, rectangular houses located mostly inside the fort walls. Archeological studies found evidence of human existence on the land as early as 8,500 years ago. The shallow ford allowed easy crossing of the river for trade and hunting. Today, the surrounding fields on the Virginia side are planted with soybean plants, which glow with shades of gold in the fall season.

KERRY FARAONE

Purcellville, Virginia

Confluence

The confluence of the Shenandoah and Potomac Rivers is a breathtaking natural landmark located at Harpers Ferry, West Virginia, where the two rivers meet at the borders of Virginia, West Virginia, and Maryland. The Shenandoah River, flowing from the western slopes of the Blue Ridge Mountains, merges with the Potomac River, which carves its way through rugged cliffs and scenic valleys. This meeting point is marked by dramatic landscapes of steep rock formations, lush green forests, and wide riverbanks. The confluence holds significant historical and cultural importance for Virginia and the broader region. It served as a key geographic and transportation hub during the colonial and Civil War eras. The confluence also remains vital to Virginia's natural heritage and tourism, providing opportunities for outdoor recreation such as hiking, fishing, and kayaking, and drawing visitors to Harpers Ferry National Historical Park and to the Appalachian Trail, which crosses the Potomac at this location. The rivers contribute to the region's ecosystems, supporting diverse wildlife and water resources for communities downstream.

KERRY FARAONE
Purcellville, Virginia

Blue Ridge Mountains

The Blue Ridge Mountains, a prominent section of the Appalachian Mountain range, stretch across Virginia and West Virginia, offering stunning landscapes and rich biodiversity. Renowned for their rolling hills, misty vistas, and vibrant fall foliage, these mountains are home to Shenandoah National Park and the Blue Ridge Parkway, two iconic attractions. Ecologically, the Blue Ridge Mountains support diverse plant and animal life, including many endemic species, and serve as a vital watershed for surrounding regions. Culturally and historically, they have shaped the heritage of Virginia and West Virginia, with deep ties to Appalachian traditions, music, and early settlement patterns. They also play a significant economic role, drawing millions of visitors annually for hiking, camping, and scenic exploration, boosting tourism in both states.

CATHY GARDNER
Rockingham, Virginia

Log Cabin

This structure, a log cabin located on private property in the Shenandoah Valley, exemplifies just one of the many types of cabins built in Virginia. Log cabins were built by different ethnic groups, as can be seen in construction techniques and materials analogous to the builder's regional origins. Due to the challenges of settling in the American colonies, the successful construction of these homes often necessitated sharing architectural methods used by different groups that had immigrated to the American colonies.

ROBERTA GELLNER
Saint Marys, West Virginia

Virginia Gardens

This piece was inspired by the colonial gardens of Virginia in Williamsburg, at Monticello, and at Mount Vernon. Early Virginia statesmen were avid gardeners who cultivated flowers and vegetables. This practice continues to be celebrated at those locations as well as at the Norfolk Botanical Gardens and Lewis Ginter Botanical Gardens. Historic Garden Week is held in April each year, when private gardens are opened to be enjoyed by the public. This event began in 1927 as a way to raise funds to save trees that had been planted by Thomas Jefferson at Monticello. Virginia gardens dramatically change with Virginia's four seasons; they serve as a backdrop for weddings and family celebrations. They also serve as classrooms for educating botanists as we seek to develop new plant varieties for their beauty, climate resilience, and disease resistance.

PRISCILLA GODFREY
Philomont, Virginia

Charles Hamilton Houston Courthouse

Here, in 1933, Charles Houston and several members of the Howard University faculty litigated the defense of a Black man charged with the murder of two white women in Middleburg. It was the first time a Black attorney insisted that the legal team be made up of Black attorneys. At that time, only 58 of Virginia's 2,500 attorneys were Black. The case is also known for helping to end the practice of seating all-white juries. Houston had identified thirteen Black property owners, craftsmen, and businessmen who were qualified but excluded from consideration from jury service, setting up a federal appeal. Most remarkable was Houston's closing argument before an all-white jury, who agreed on a sentence of life imprisonment instead of electrocution. Houston went on to fight against separate-but-equal school education and many other civil rights denied to African American people. The courthouse was renamed the Charles Hamilton Houston Courthouse to honor his accomplishments.

PRISCILLA GODFREY
Philomont, Virginia

Indian Mound Cemetery

The Indian Mound Cemetery in Romney, West Virginia, is unique; it has graves from the Revolutionary War, the Civil War, and the Vietnam War. However, the most remarkable feature is the Indian mound. It was customary for Indigenous people to bury their dead after battles in a mound. In the mid-1800s, this Indian mound was on the property of David Gibson and his Sycamore Dale plantation. In 1860, he conveyed the land to the City of Romney on the condition that the mound was never disturbed. Subsequently, in 1903 he donated 5 acres to the Indian Mound Cemetery Company for use as a burial site for white people. This cemetery contains the first memorial to the Confederate dead, which was added on Sept. 26, 1867. Recently, efforts are being made by Indigenous people to locate artifacts and mounds to ensure that they are not taken, moved, or disturbed.

GWEN GOEPEL
Floyd, Virginia

Blue Ridge Parkway: Tuggle's Gap

Passing by MP165 on the Blue Ridge Parkway, drivers see a historic roadside inn, a 1938 landmark, that was built in anticipation of the construction of the Blue Ridge Parkway. The National Park Service built the scenic parkway through parts of the Appalachian Mountains, traversing several distinct geological areas along its nearly 500-mile length. The natural beauty of the winding roads is enhanced by an outstanding collection of stone-faced bridges, which are an important part of the parkway's design concept and the most distinctive feature of the Blue Ridge Parkway. These structures had to be functionally and visually appropriate, blending well with the mountain landscape.

GWEN GOEPEL
Floyd, Virginia

DC (Dad's Cabin)

My husband has long admired log cabins as representing the strength and spirit of the true Appalachian pioneer. He was fascinated with researching them and was amazed by the fact that two experienced woodsmen could go into the woods with little more than axes to construct a strong, weather-resistant structure. He challenged himself to build his own cabin without power, using only vintage tools and a few he had made himself. Preferring to work alone, he built a gin pole to assist him in lifting the 18- and 22-foot-long logs. The foundation was built from stones on our land. He constructed windows and a chestnut door, using no metal whatsoever. The ancient presence of peace and tranquility in DC, nestled in the land's beautiful patchwork of fields, woods, and water, will surely be appreciated by family and friends for generations to come.

CAROLYN GOINS
Hamilton, Virginia

August Court Days

The Leesburg County Courthouse was the site of all legal affairs in the county. It also gave the county residents a place and time to join together for discussions and activities of social and significant importance. In Loudoun County, Virginia, a judge arrived in August each year. The purpose was to adjudicate the legal needs of the people: criminal, wills, or filing of land exchanges. Because of this, Leesburg assumed a festival atmosphere each August.

PAULA GOLDEN
Blacksburg, Virginia

Spirit of the Blue Ridge

This quilt celebrates the spirit of the Monacan peoples in Ellett Valley, Virginia. As the Spirit walks the land of this area, one feels things traditionally considered female, life giving, and providing, the glory of the mountains, treachery and abundance from the rivers, and the hardships and grief of senseless deaths, among the heritages of many. For each step that is walked, a story lies beneath. This whole-cloth quilt is made from a vintage tablecloth that was dyed with indigo. The embroidered design is evocative of embroidered "slips" that were featured on the early quilts in Virginia. The placement of the tablecloth's embroidered pattern spoke to me of a creative being.

SANDI GOLDMAN
Annandale, Virginia

Historic Green Spring Gardens

Located in Fairfax County, this site is home to a historic estate with a rich and layered past. Before European settlement, the land that became Green Spring was part of a region inhabited by Indigenous peoples, particularly the Doeg tribe. The centerpiece of the property is a brick house built in 1784 by John Moss, a justice of the county court and a Revolutionary War veteran who served under George Washington. The house originally stood on 540 acres and functioned as a working farm. Moss and his sons maintained the farm, and like many landowners at the time, he enslaved individuals to labor on the property. Following occupation of several other landowners over time, eventually the site was donated to the Fairfax County Park Authority, ensuring its preservation for future generations. Today the gardens encompasses 31 acres and serves as a vibrant public park. It is a beloved destination for nature lovers and history enthusiasts alike.

MARIANNE GRAVELY
Virginia Beach, Virginia

Yellow Lotus

Nelumbo lutea, or yellow lotus, is native to the Sandbridge area of Virginia Beach and can be found in the Lotus Garden Park. The flowers grow from June to September, with each blossom blooming for just three days. This pond full of blooming lotuses is beloved by visitors to nearby Sandbridge. The yellow lotus was once relied on as food by the region's native tribes. The large, starchy roots were dug up and baked like sweet potatoes, a key source of sustenance during the winter. The leaves and shoots were eaten like greens, the unripe seeds tasted like chestnuts, and the ripe seeds were hulled and roasted, ground into flour, or eaten like nuts. Native Americans expanded the plant's range northward by carrying it as a food source. These beautiful flowers were once abundant in the park and were celebrated by an annual lotus festival from 1955 to 2019. While they are still a treat to see, their numbers have diminished over the years.

JODY GRUENDEL
Williamsburg, Virginia

Underground Majesty

Geologists believe that Virginia caves began forming millions of years ago. Archeological studies show that Native Americans explored and utilized caves in southwestern Virginia almost 10,000 years ago. It's also documented that George Washington and Thomas Jefferson explored Virginia's caves. If you've ever visited Virginia's Southwest or Shenandoah Valley caves, then you may have been awestruck by their beauty and how they were created. Today, spelunking, the recreational exploration of wild cave systems, is a favorite pastime here.

HEIDI HAYNES
Winchester, Virginia

Old Jake—Iconic Winchester

Old Jake is a historic weather vane that sits atop Rouss Fire Hall. It is an iconic piece of folk art that adorns the Winchester skyline and is a popular subject of local artists. Made by a local carriage maker, George Barnhart, who named it after his son Jacob, the weather vane was installed on the Union Firehall in 1860. It was later moved to the current building in 1895.

LYN COLEMAN
Moneta, Virginia

Fawn Hiding in the Meadow

Although Virginia has excellent habitat for deer, early overhunting by white settlers decimated the herds. Since the 1930s, game laws have protected and even restocked the whitetail deer population. Numbers have benefited by native habitat restoration and tighter hunting and harvesting laws. Whitetail fawns are born in the spring, and the mothers hide them from predators. The whitetail deer is native to Virginia, and as the largest native herbivore it has a great impact on the ecosystem.

BARBARA HOLLINGER
Vienna, Virginia

Basalt Column Tower or Catoctin Basalt Columns

Just a short hike off the Appalachian Trail near Compton Gap in Shenandoah National Park, basalt columns remain as a reminder of the remarkable history of Virginia's Blue Ridge Mountains. More than 500,000 years ago, long before humans inhabited Virginia, the supercontinent Rodinia rifted apart, separating what are now North America and Europe. The rapid continental shift caused lava flows to pour over the surface, covering large regions, including Appalachia. As the magma cooled, columnar jointing formations were created on both sides of what is now the Atlantic Ocean, and they are still visible today. The geology of the region is unique and plays an important part in our region's history, agriculture, and natural resources.

BARB HOLLINGER
Vienna, Virginia

Sky Magic: Northern Lights over Northern Virginia

A perhaps once-in-a-lifetime glimpse of the aurora borealis over the rolling hills of Northern Virginia is captured in improvisational piecing. The spike in solar storms on October 10, 2024, and new technology in digital photography allowed the northern lights to surpass viewers' expectations even south of the fortieth parallel.

ELLEN BRERETON ICOCHEA
Springfield, Virginia

National Museum of the Marine Corps: Celebrating 250 Years, 1775–2025

This quilt honors the outstanding museum located in Triangle, Virginia. The soaring architecture is built to depict the now-iconic flag-raising scene on Iwo Jima during World War II, immortalized in Joe Rosenthal's iconic photograph, a scene also depicted at the U.S. Marine Corps War Memorial in Arlington, Virginia. The museum, which opened in 2006, is a 240,000-square-foot structure situated on a 135-acre site adjacent to Marine Corps Base Quantico, Virginia. The property also includes the 23.3-acre Semper Fidelis Memorial Park, lined with 30,000 commemorative bricks, and includes Semper Fidelis Memorial Chapel. The museum honors the commitment, accomplishments, and sacrifices of all US Marines. I made this quilt to honor my husband, Sergeant George A. Icochea, and family members Corporal Calixto Cornier and Lance Corporal Anthony Hernandez.

KAREN JOHNSTON
Fallbrook, California

Shenandoah Salamander

Endemic to Shenandoah National Park, the endangered Shenandoah salamander represents the fragility of the balance of nature and the impact of climate change. The phrase "power of place" usually refers to the human species and their relationship with the environment. In this case, the species is an amphibian, and the environment is high in the mountains, with significant cloud cover. This salamander is found only on the tops of three mountains in Shenandoah National Park. They depend on a moist and cool environment, but the habitat available to them is shrinking as the local climate gets warmer and drier. They are essentially trapped in their current location, since they would not survive an exodus through the drier, warmer climate at lower elevations in the park.

SUSANNE MILLER JONES
Potomac Falls, Virginia

Grand Illumination—Williamsburg

Each December, Williamsburg, Virginia, provides two simultaneous eighteenth-century-style fireworks displays on the three Saturdays before Christmas. The celebration is based on the colonial custom of illuminating public buildings to honor a sovereign's birthday or a victory in battle. The Colonial Williamsburg Fifes and Drums entertain revelers throughout the streets. The festivities include musicians, performers, community groups, puppeteers, and storytellers. Williamsburg was the former colonial capital of Virginia. Williamsburg's decorations for Christmas and its celebration of the Christmas season attract many visitors to the historic town each year.

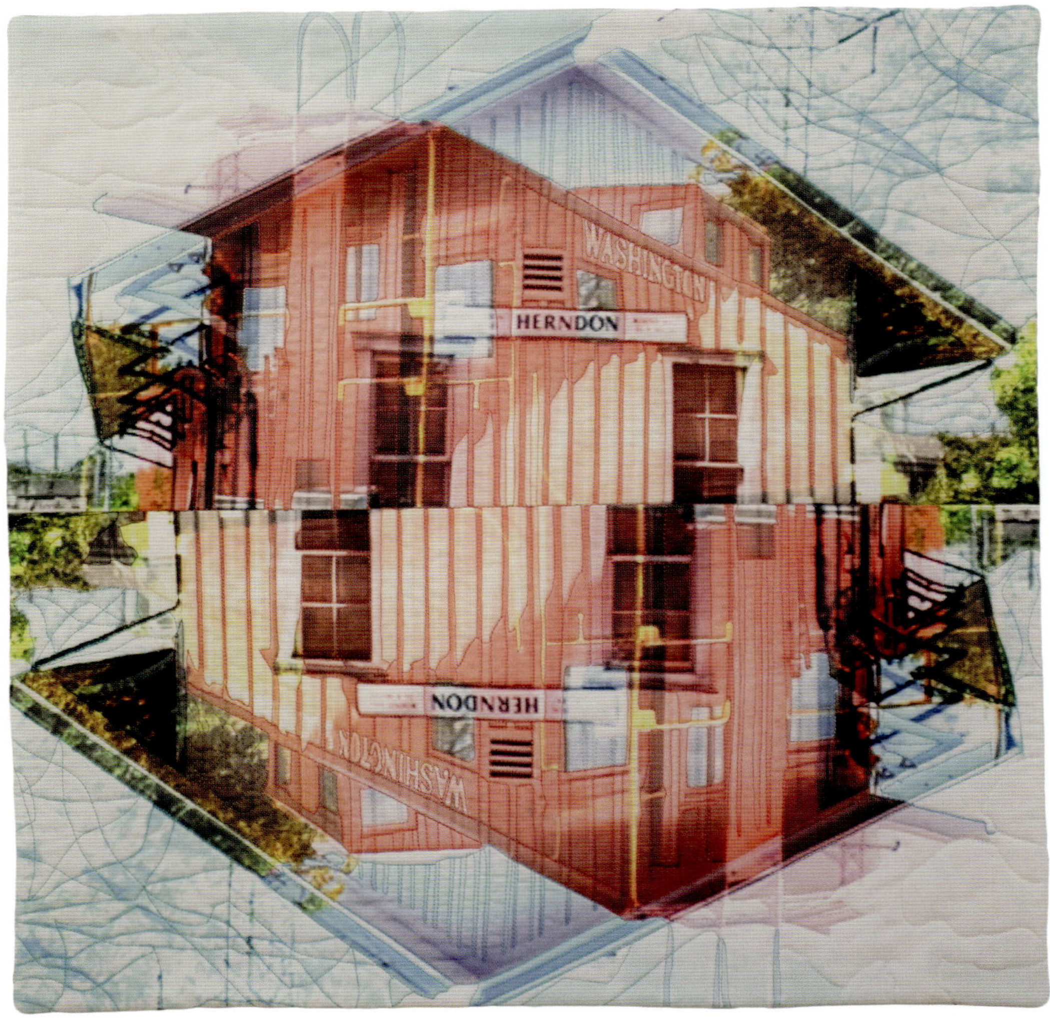

SUSANNE MILLER JONES
Potomac Falls, Virginia

Herndon, Virginia

The train depot opened in the Herndon area before the town was an entity. It allowed local dairy farmers to ship milk to Alexandria, Georgetown, and Washington. Businesses grew up around the depot, servicing the farmers, stimulating the area's development, and giving birth to the town of Herndon.

SUSANNE MILLER JONES
Potomac Falls, Virginia

Tiger Swallowtail

The eastern tiger swallowtail, one of our largest butterflies, is the state insect of Virginia. They live primarily in deciduous woodlands and are one of the most common butterflies on the East Coast. Female swallowtails lay their eggs on the leaves of woody plants. They feed on nectar from wildflowers and other flowers in neighborhood gardens from spring through fall. The butterfly in this piece is landing on a coneflower.

BUNNIE JORDAN
Vienna, Virginia

Korean Bell Garden

Located in Fairfax, the Korean Bell Garden was unveiled in 2011. It serves as a cultural landmark for Korean Americans and is the only garden of its kind in the entire western hemisphere. It is also the only public Korean Bell Pavilion on the East Coast.

MARY KERR
Woodbridge, Virginia

Virginia's Music Road

Southwestern Virginia is home to a diverse musical heritage that includes Appalachian, folk, and bluegrass music. Bluegrass greats Ralph Stanley, the Carter family, and Jim and Jesse McReynolds were a few of the pioneers in their field that inspired others to share their love of music and their culture. In 2004 the Crooked Road was designated as Virginia's Heritage Music Trail. It connects sixty unique venues as it winds through 333 miles of beautiful landscape. This quilt features a vintage top dated circa 1910, vintage rickrack, and fragments of a vintage shirt that celebrates bluegrass music.

AMY LEMMONS
Harrisonburg, Virginia

Chesapecten jeffersonius

Chesapecten jeffersonius was designated Virginia's state fossil in 1993. A drawing of this scallop shell found on Virginia's coastal plain was the first North American fossil to appear in scientific literature in 1687, but the fossils date to the Pliocene era, about four million years ago. The 8-inch diameter of the quilt's shell approximates the actual size of the fossil specimen.

Shenandoah Mountain National Scenic Area

This area lies in Augusta, Highland, and Rockingham Counties in the George Washington National Forest of Virginia. Apart from beautiful scenery, the area provides clean drinking water for multiple municipalities and is the only known habitat for the Cow Knob salamander. Lynn Cameron has long been an ambassador for this region. She has spent the last twenty years working tirelessly to protect the area through her work with the Virginia Wilderness Committee and Friends of the Shenandoah Mountain. These collaborations have ensured the protection of diverse plant and wildlife habitat, clean water for communities downstream, and a variety of recreational opportunities.

LYNN LOTHMAN
Leesburg, Virginia

Dog Money: Leesburg, Virginia

This piece features the Loudoun Museum, the Potomac, the people, and the famous dog money that was the currency of Leesburg during the Civil War years. Leesburg is an important place in the history of the Civil War, partly because the Potomac was the boundary between the North and the South and the people caught in the middle. Because of its strategic location, it became a coveted spot both for the Confederate and Union forces. As a result, Leesburg was estimated to have changed hands 150 times during the four years of Civil War, and each changeover brought in different types of money. In 1861, the town of Leesburg chose to issue its own municipal currency so that business in the town would not be interrupted with each takeover. These bills featured George Washington, Lady Liberty, and an American water spaniel dog. Thus it became known as "dog money."

LEAH MARKOV-LINDSEY
Austin, Texas

On the Shoulders of Giants (Virginia)

The individuals whose names I have included in this quilt were enslaved by my eighth-great-grandfather Samuel Brockman, who was a tobacco planter in Spotsylvania and Orange Counties, Virginia. I believe the institution of slavery cannot be separated from the history of our nation, especially in Virginia, where so many of the enslaved toiled primarily on tobacco plantations. We sometimes cursorily acknowledge this part of our country, but I hope that by claiming my history as a descendant of enslavers and engaging in conversations with those who view my project and choose to engage with the work, I may take a step toward apologizing for the deep harm my family, including those in Virginia, has inflicted on Africans and Black Americans.

JANET ACUFF MARNEY
Fairfax, Virginia

The Sand Cave

The Sand Cave is nestled high in the Appalachian Mountains near Cumberland Gap, Virginia. Unlike most caves, the floor of this cave is all sand, and the roof contains fossils of ancient sea creatures. About 350 million years ago, the entire area was covered by sea water! The ongoing effects of weather eventually eroded this giant sandstone boulder, leaving a 250-foot-wide opening. The 4-mile trail to the cave begins in Ewing, near the home of my maternal grandparents. It is a truly unique and special place.

SANDY MAXFIELD
Raleigh, North Carolina

Shenandoah Sunset

This quilt is inspired by a sunset view from Skyline Drive. Shenandoah National Park, created in 1935, spans the spine of the Blue Ridge Mountains and attracts more than 1.4 million visitors a year. The park provides a glorious natural environment for wilderness and recreational activities. Of course, history in the area goes back much further than the history of the park. Skyline Drive follows the crest of the Blue Ridge, which is part of the Appalachian chain dating back over a billion years. Native people began visiting the area eight thousand to nine thousand years ago for seasonal hunting and gathering and to find sources of stone for tools and weapons. Europeans arrived about three hundred years ago.

SUZANNE MEADER
Sterling, Virginia

Presidents Park, Williamsburg, Virginia

Presidents Park in Williamsburg, Virginia, no longer exits. The brainchild of Everette H. "Haley" Newman II, a local entrepreneur, and sculptor David Adickes, this outdoor museum was constructed in 2004 and went bankrupt in 2010. In 2012 the sculptures were set to be demolished. The contractor hired to demolish the sculptures elected to save them instead, and so he moved them to his private property. This was no small task, since the sculptures range in size from 15 to 18 feet tall each and are made of concrete. The warehoused "heads" garnered interest from folks and have become an attraction for professional and amateur photographers. Oddly, the setting where the sculptures now reside is overgrown and marginally maintained, and it mimics an abandoned cemetery for these decaying sculptures. The area provides an interesting tribute to some of the men who led our democracy.

SUZANNE MEADER
Sterling, Virginia

Tangier Island Crab Shanty

Tangier is a remote island located 12 miles from the shore in the Chesapeake Bay, off the coast of Virginia. This island is only 1.5 miles long and was discovered by Europeans in 1608. The island is accessible only by air or sea, and crabbing, fishing, and oyster industries have been a way of life on Tangier for hundreds of years. Colorful crab shanties pepper the coastline and are the emblem of this small, hardworking, and vibrant community where residents have a passion for the seafood industry. Signature crab shanties are used by local watermen as a place to rest during their long days, where they can sort through the day's catch and prep their harvest for sale.

AYNEX MERCADO
Frederick, Maryland

Cursing Neptune

In an effort to ensure that Virginia Beach is a family-friendly vacation destination, in the 1990s the town posted several "No Cursing" signs. There was a fine levied of $250 per incident, and more than $6,000 was collected from infractions. The "No Cursing" signs are an interesting and unique aspect of the history of Virginia Beach, as is the statue of King Neptune. Due to difficulties with demands of free speech and fair application of this law, the signs were removed from the area in 2019, then subsequently auctioned off by the police foundation.

JANE MILLER
Moseley, Virginia

Polegreen Meeting House

Located in Hanover County, Polegreen is one of four original meetinghouses that were permitted during early colonization. Many folks may not realize that "freedom of religion" was not guaranteed for the first 170 years of our nation. Therefore, under the king's rule, colonists were required to attend regular worship under the Anglican Church, paying stiff penalties for any absenteeism or other misdeeds. During the "Great Awakening" in the 1730s, a young Presbyterian minister named Samuel Davies arrived from Pennsylvania. Given permission by Governor Gooch, Rev. Davies became the first to legally preach to the colonists in central Virginia. Polegreen, named after the original land-grant owner, attracted many worshipers. Young Patrick Henry and his mother were among the crowds. Enslaved people were welcomed to worship with the group and were often given reading lessons from the Bible.

ROXZANNA MONTAGUE
Roseland, Virginia

Daniel Boone Crossing the Cumberland Gap

The Cumberland Gap has played an important role in Virginia's history since prehistoric times. Buffalo used to migrate through the gap on yearly migrations. It was an essential trade route to the Mississippian people as far back as 1200 CE. There is archeological evidence dating back to between 2000 and 4000 BCE of people using the Cumberland Gap. In 1775, Daniel Boone blazed a trail through the Cumberland Gap. Nearly 300,000 people followed Boone to settle west, forever changing southwestern Virginia and beyond.

Jackson Ferry Shot Tower

The Tower, built in 1807, is a well-recognized landmark in Wythe County, Virginia. It is so iconic that it is featured on the county seal. It is one of only three shot towers left standing in the US and is unique among those for its shorter height and building material. The tower is 75 feet tall, and the only one built of limestone instead of brick, allowing the interior to stay at a consistently cooler temperature to create superior shot. This tower illustrates the ingenuity of early southwestern Virginia pioneers. Their supply of lead shot played a vital role in the lives of early settlers exploring the frontier.

CAROL MONTI
Blacksburg, Virginia

Merry Oak

This particular ancient white oak grew for centuries near the Smithfield Plantation house in Blacksburg. The tree is considered a "Witness Tree," since it was present since before colonial times and witnessed the life of plantation families and all that has happened since. The Merry Oak became a sacred place to generations of enslaved people of Smithfield Plantation. Oral history passed down through the descendants tells of the enslaved gathering under the tree to share stories, celebrate life events, and hold religious ceremonies. The 350-to-400-year-old tree collapsed in 2020 due to old age, but its remnants are still treasured by the descendants of the enslaved. The plantation house at Smithfield was built by Col. William Preston and his wife, Susanna. The Preston family included three Virginia governors, who were born there. Completed in 1774, the well-preserved house sits adjacent to the Virginia Tech campus in Blacksburg. While the history of the Preston family is well documented, that of the enslaved families is less known. Many descendants of the formerly enslaved families describe a connection to their ancestors that can be felt through the Merry Oak.

CARLY MUL
Hamilton, Virginia

Luray Caverns

One day in 1878, a few friends were walking in a field when suddenly, on the very hot summer day, they felt a blast of cold air coming up from the ground from what was a limestone sinkhole. They dug for four hours and couldn't believe what was revealed. Now you can visit this popular natural wonder, located west of the central part of Shenandoah National Park, where caverns are 260 feet below the surface. Several bodies of water are in the caverns. The underground temperature is always 54 degrees; the popular walk into the caverns is half a mile long. These are the largest caverns on the East Coast. The only creatures living in the caverns are trilobites, which inhabit the areas in complete darkness.

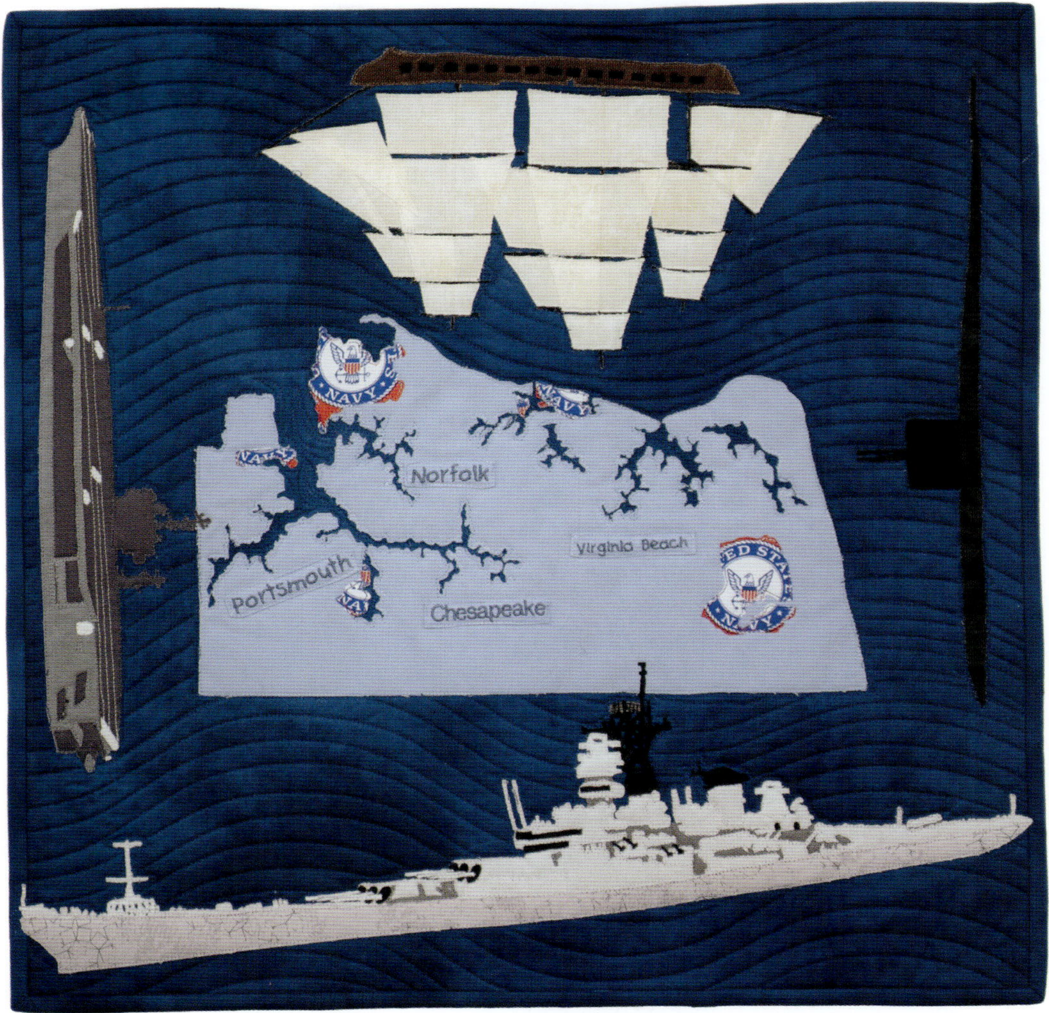

LAURA NELSON
Norfolk, Virginia

Ships of Norfolk

Naval Station Norfolk is the largest naval base in the world. It has played a significant role in US history. Originally built as Gosport Shipyard by a British merchant in 1767 for ship repairs, and then taken over by the Virginia Colonial Navy, it was destroyed by the British during the Revolutionary War. It was restored by the US government but later was set on fire three times by Union and Confederate forces during the Civil War. It officially became home to the US Navy in 1917. Both the size and purpose of the naval base have expanded over time, and it now includes services of amphibious training, intelligence, submarines, air station, and reserve forces, among others. NATO US headquarters was established in 1952 on the base. The first US battleship, cruiser, and aircraft carrier were built at this station, and currently over 75 ships and 134 aircraft are based there.

MARIETTA NESTER
Montvale, Virginia

Falling Springs Falls

Falling Springs Falls, Virginia, is a powerful place that captures the soul and imagination. The soft mists rising throughout the landscape during a light rain intermix with the mists created by the waterfall itself. It is located in Bath County near the border of Virginia and West Virginia.

MARIETTA NESTER
Montvale, Virginia

Peaks of Otter

The Peaks of Otter has served as a landmark since the time Indigenous people lived in this area of Virginia. Early European settlers found the Peaks to be a place to homestead and grow their crops, animals, and families. It is now a destination spot with a park, picnic area, campground, and lodge. Today the parkway system brings visitors to hike or to take in the evening sunset over the lake. This view is from Cedar Hills Farm, which is a popular wedding destination.

JOHANNA NORRY
Avondale Estates, Georgia

The Great Dismal Swamp

In his 1962 book *The Great Dismal Swamp*, Hubert J. Davis wrote, "This book was written for those who think of the Dismal Swamp as a hostile filthy mire, teeming with poisonous snakes, and cloaked in mystery and misunderstanding. It was also written for school children so that they may escape such false notions and really appreciate the Dismal Swamp for what it is. For those who really know the swamp, the bird lover, nature lover, sportsman, boatman and scientist, it is unsurpassed in natural beauty and opportunities by any similar area in the United States." There is a legend called "The Tale of the Frustrated Witch" in Davis's book that captured my imagination as a child. The tale describes a witch who tormented hunters in the Dismal Swamp until a spell was cast on her by a hunter's Indian guide, and she was turned into a stump. According to Davis, you can still find the witchlike stump near the east shore of Lake Drummond.

KATHLEEN O'LEARY
Burke, Virginia

We Will Provide

St. Mary of Sorrows Catholic Church in Fairfax Station, Virginia, was built by Irish immigrants and dedicated in 1860. It was used as a hospital by Clara Barton and other brave women who took care of wounded soldiers in 1862, transported by the railroad located nearby. Today the church supports many community outreach programs.

CAROL AND GENE OLIVER
Martinsburg, West Virginia

Lewis Manor House

Here is the Lewis House at Fort Lewis Lodge. The house, which was built in the early 1800s, is located on the site of Fort Lewis, a frontier fort during the French and Indian War. The area around Fort Lewis has been identified as one of the earliest colonial settlements formed when the area of western Virginia that is now Bath County was settled in the 1740s. Remarkably, the original 950-acre tract that the house stands on has remained intact since it was surveyed for John Lewis in 1746.

HOLLY PANZERA
Williamsburg, Virginia

Ginkgo Grove

Located within the Blandy Experimental Farm at the State Arboretum in Boyce, Virginia, are more than three hundred ginkgo trees, creating one of the largest public ginkgo groves in America. A popular time to visit is in the fall, when the unique leaves turn a brilliant gold. Ginkgo trees are living fossils, dating back millions of years. They have survived numerous geological events and even outlived the dinosaurs. They provide a glimpse into the earth's history, serving as a living link between our present and the distant past. Ginkgo trees also offer a range of practical benefits. Their leaves, seeds, and extracts have been used in traditional medicine for centuries, and various health benefits are attributed to them.

HOLLY PANZERA
Williamsburg, Virginia

The Starving Time

The Starving Time in Jamestown, Virginia, occurred during the winter of 1609–1610. Following the drought and crop failure of 1609, Jamestown's earliest settlers suffered from a food shortage, impure water, and a siege by Powhatan warriors. There were five hundred residents at the beginning of the winter. By the spring of 1610, only sixty-one remained. *The Starving Time* reflects the ultimate sacrifice of the earliest European settlers.

SARA RAYAPROL
Warrenton, Virginia

The Flying Circus Airshow in Bealeton, Virginia

This is my rendering of the Flying Circus Airshow in Bealeton, which is one of a kind. On my work, the crowd is entertained by a wing walker doing daring maneuvers on a 1939 WACO UPF-7 as the hot-air balloons float through the sky. This show has been held since 1970 and is the longest continually running air show in Virginia and perhaps even in the world. Performances occur every weekend from May through October, thrilling audiences with formation-flying demonstrations, world-class acrobatics, death-defying wing walkers, and classic comedy routines. The airplanes at the circus include Stearmans, WACOs, Fleets, Cubs, Champs, and others from the world war eras. This air show embodies Virginians' courage, innovation, and pioneering spirit.

SARA RAYAPROL
Warrenton, Virginia

The Stone House: Then and Now

The historic Stone House is located in Manassas National Battlefield Park. This house was captured by Union soldiers during the First Battle of Manassas in 1861. The structure's sturdy stone walls, the nearby well, and its proximity to the main road leading to DC hospitals made it an ideal field hospital for the Union forces. This piece depicts a then-and-now concept, with the ghostly wagon on the left reflecting its use during the Civil War, and the modern car showing that the house is currently positioned on Route 29. National Park Service volunteers share its history and stories of wounded soldiers who were sheltered there.

SHARON REZIN
Middletown, Virginia

Silver Lake Mill

The Silver Lake Mill was first built in 1822, and it milled grain for the local community for more than 170 years, before closing in 1996. During that time, the building burned down in the 1850s and again during the Civil War in 1864. In 2024 it became the home of the Virginia Quilt Museum.

NANCY ROCHE
Waynesboro, Virginia

Lighthouses of Mathews County

Mathews County is home to two distinct lighthouses. Each has historical significance and represents a unique method of protection for seagoing vessels. The New Point Comfort Lighthouse is the third-oldest lighthouse on the Chesapeake Bay and was commissioned in 1804 by Thomas Jefferson. Originally it sat on the end of the southernmost peninsula of Mathews County. In 1933, a hurricane separated the area of the lighthouse from the mainland, and the lighthouse has been standing on a small island ever since. It is a popular tourist location in Mathews County. The current Wolf Trap Lighthouse was first lit in 1894 and is one of only about eleven lighthouses of its type in the country. In 2017, it was taken out of service and was sold. It is now in private ownership and is being restored.

CRYSTAL ROUSSEAU
Stafford, Virginia

Most Haunted Road in Virginia

It is said that Elbow Road is the most haunted road in Virginia. The very curvy road is only two lanes, the speed limit is 45 mph, and shoulders are either sparse or nonexistent. So many fatal accidents have occurred that people go out of their way, day or night, to avoid the road entirely. Although attempts have been made to make the road safer, it remains dangerous. Besides unnerving road conditions, it is said that haunted ghosts of those who have passed away on this road continue to make appearances. Some believe that seeing these ghosts has actually caused accidents. One legend has it that if you park your car on the side of the road in the dark (do not attempt this), and you sit on the hood and wait, you'll see the muddy wet footprints of a little girl coming in your direction . . .

CRYSTAL ROUSSEAU
Stafford, Virginia

Neptune

Dedicated in 2005 at the annual Neptune Festival Boardwalk Weekend in Virginia Beach, the 34-foot-tall bronze sculpture of King Neptune was created by Paul DePasquale. Funded by private donations, the statue weighs 12.5 tons and is surrounded by dolphins, a turtle, and an octopus.

LUANA RUBIN
Boulder, Colorado

Assateague Pony at Sunrise

As a girl, I was captivated by Marguerite Henry's *Misty of Chincoteague*. That is what inspired this piece, expressing the joy of a girl's first horse love, with colors expressing happiness of simpler times. This breed is classified as a pony because they are short and stocky. They are thought to be descendants of the survivors of a Spanish galleon that sank off the coast of Assateague. Two herds make their home on Assateague. The Maryland herd is managed by the National Park Service, and the Virginia herd by the Chincoteague Volunteer Fire Department. Thousands of visitors come to the annual event, when the ponies swim from Assateague to Chincoteague at the end of July.

RICKI SELVA
Gig Harbor, Washington

The Appalachian Trail

Challenge, solace, camaraderie, solitude: The Appalachian National Scenic Trail offers a wide range of experiences to those seeking its treasures. The Trail is the longest hiking-only footpath in the world, and Virginia is home to a quarter of its miles, more than any other state. Thru-hikers find themselves reaching Virginia as forest leaves burst forth, obscuring views, and so the trail becomes a "Green Tunnel." Thru-hikers suffer the notorious "Virginia Blues" as a physical journey turns inward and becomes a voyage of self-discovery. To walk the Appalachian Trail is to walk through history. Stone fences, collier pits, foundations, chimneys, and headstones remind us that we are crossing paths with ancestors who left their mark, as well as ancestors who tread so lightly as to leave no mark upon the land. In 2020, my husband and I walked the entire 2,193 miles of the Appalachian Trail to celebrate our new life in retirement.

RICKI SELVA
Gig Harbor, Washington

Paint Lick Mountain Pictographs

Even though Virginia has been inhabited for tens of thousands of years, most of those inhabitants left no evidence of their time in this land. Paint Lick Mountain is one of several rare exceptions. Pictographs painted by using local iron oxide deposits sit at the edge of a quartzite escarpment atop a mountain that takes its name from those deposits. The images on this stone face depict birds and other creatures, human forms, and some more-abstract figures. In spite of weathering and vandalism, the pictographs remain. They are located on private property and are not accessible by the public, and they are on the National Register of Historic Places as well as the Virginia Landmarks Register.

PAM SHANLEY
Summerville, South Carolina

Cascading Power

There is nothing like a waterfall to make you feel powerful! The mere act of the water finding its own way through the mountains and valleys and finally spilling out in full glory exhibits a freedom and a desire to survive. For me, living in Virginia reflects that freedom. Historically, Virginia is home to many of our country's founders. Environmentally, Virginia reminds us of the fragility of nature and how we need to preserve that glory. Reaching Cascade Falls in Pembroke causes us to reflect on our own freedoms and know how important it is to pass that on to our children. We are reminded of power and beauty and perseverance. When we diligently climb to reach the falls, we are rewarded.

SHERYL SIMS
Alexandria, Virginia

Christ Church, Old Town Alexandria, Virginia

Christ Church is in Old Town Alexandria. The church where George Washington once worshiped, it is a religious institution of pride for city leaders and citizens who attend. There are numerous historical plaques and burial sites on the lovely grounds. Two of George Washington's pallbearers are buried on the grounds. It has a long history of Christian education and fellowship for the ever-growing congregation; it is now the church home to many Alexandria families, including members of Daughters of the King, an international religious order of lay women.

SHERYL SIMS
Alexandria, Virginia

Woodlawn Plantation

Woodlawn Plantation is located on lands first inhabited by the Doeg people and was later part of George Washington's Mount Vernon Plantation. In 1805, Nelly Custis, granddaughter of Gen. Washington, was given the plantation as a wedding gift. Antislavery Quakers purchased Woodlawn in the 1840s. This group worked with a well-established free Black community, and together they demonstrated that with agricultural reform and Black landownership, Virginia could be successfully cultivated without slavery. Woodlawn was the home of Chalkley Gillingham, my Quaker ancestor.

PAT SLOAN
Herndon, Virginia

You Can Always Find the Way

Shenandoah National Park is a treasured gem in Virginia. The Wilderness Act, established in 1964, offers protection for public lands so they will remain untouched. It is both inspiring and humbling to witness land that remains in its natural state. Not far from this location is Big Meadows, an exceptional site to explore another of the park's diverse landscapes. That distinctive high-elevation meadow is a surprise to find in the woods and provides wonderful hiking opportunities. This piece shows the compass located at the visitor center. Like many of the navigation markers throughout the park, it is crafted from natural material and reveals the marks of countless visitors over the years.

LISA STEGELAND
Williamsburg, Virginia

Godspeed

On December 6, 1606, 104 men set out on a journey traveling on the *Susan Constant*, *Godspeed*, and *Discovery* from England, which eventually led to the settlement of Jamestown, Virginia, in 1607, the first permanent English settlement in North America. The settlement of Jamestown and its successes as well as the hardships that were endured there played an important role in the colonization of Virginia and America.

POLLY STOUT
Little River, South Carolina

A Place Growing Up

Meem's Bottom-Covered Bridge is Virginia's only historic, one-lane, drivable covered bridge. Constructed in 1893, it is a 204-foot-long span over the Shenandoah River. It has two burr arch trusses and stone abutments from local quarries that extend 10 feet below the riverbed. It was built by a local apple orchard owner for transporting apples to market. Did you know that covered bridges are also known as kissing bridges for young lovers?

CINDY STOWE
Sterling, Virginia

Monticello Blossoms

The commonwealth of Virginia selected the dogwood as its state flower on March 6, 1918, and it became the state tree in 1956. The dogwood is essential to Virginia's history, since it's the only state that has the same plant as their state flower and state tree. The dogwood tree is connected to President Thomas Jefferson and his estate, Monticello. President Jefferson is one of the main reasons that the dogwood tree became popular as an ornamental tree. He loved them and promoted them for landscaping and took great pride in his own. He kept detailed records during the 1770s, and he was known to have had over 160 species of dogwoods on his estate. Monticello is a glorious sight, especially when the dogwoods are in bloom in the springtime.

PRISCILLA STULTZ
Williamsburg, Virginia

Williamsburg Winery

The Williamsburg Winery's history began in 1609, when the first settlers planted grapes on the land that is now the Wessex Hundred Farm. The winery was inspired by Europe's finest estates. It celebrated the four hundredth anniversary with the opening of the 1619 Pavilion in 2019. These days the winery hosts musical groups as well as wedding receptions and features a tasting room, hotel, and restaurant.

KARIN TAUBER
Blacksburg, Virginia

The Arrival of the *Susan Constant*

By imagining what must have been a dramatic sight for Native Americans, this piece depicts the arrival of one of the first ships to land in Virginia, with seventy-one men and young boys aboard and ready to claim their part of the New World. Jamestown, named for King James, was founded in 1607 by John Smith and other colonists, including John Rolfe. He later became the husband of Pocahontas. This became the first permanent English settlement in North America. *Susan Constant* was the largest of three ships of the English Virginia Company on the 1606–1607 voyage. After sailing back to London, the *Susan Constant* did not return to Virginia again.

KARIN TAUBER
Blacksburg, Virginia

Natural Bridge in Natural Bridge State Park

In 1774, Thomas Jefferson purchased 64 acres of land, including the 215-foot-high Natural Bridge, for twenty shillings from King George III of Great Britain. The natural arch, a limestone gorge carved out by Cedar Creek, has been a state park since 2016. In addition to the Natural Bridge, the park offers a hiking trail along the river and a model of an ancient Monacan village.

KARIN TAUBER
Blacksburg, Virginia

Sea Turtles at Virginia Coastal Waters

Chesapeake Bay and the coastal waters of Virginia are home to five of the world's seven sea turtle species. Loggerhead turtles are the most abundant. Each year between 5,000 and 10,000 sea turtles come into the Chesapeake Bay to feed. The majority of these turtles are juveniles. Adult sea turtles nest along the shores of the Barrier Islands. All sea turtle species are protected under the Endangered Species Act.

COLLEEN TAVENNER
Paw Paw, West Virginia

Paw Paw, West Virginia, Tunnel

Paw Paw, West Virginia, is named after the fruit tree. The pawpaw is a native tree and is believed to have been George Washington's favorite fruit, with its custardy inside that is a cross among a banana, mango, and a pineapple. Situated on the Potomac River near the Paw Paw Bends, Paw Paw was considered a place of strategic importance because of its proximity both to the Potomac River and the railroad during the Civil War. The town of Paw Paw became a focal point for trade and flourished, providing hundreds of jobs in leather tannery, orchards, fruit packing, and the railroads. So important was the location of the town that in 1836, the C&O Canal Co. started the construction of the Paw Paw Tunnel to try to circumvent the Paw Paw Bends on the Potomac River. Paw Paw is located on the western end of the Washington Heritage Trail.

ANNE THOMPSON
Chesapeake, Virginia

The Battle of Great Bridge

Many of us learned about the history of Lexington and Concord, but few know how important the Battle of Great Bridge was to the war for independence. The colonial victory at the Battle of Great Bridge proved that British troops could be defeated. My inspiration for the quilt is from a brief movie at the Great Bridge Battlefield and Waterways History Museum in Chesapeake, Virginia. With permission from the executive director, Elizabeth Goodwin, I took several still shots of the movie. I learned that on a cold December morning, patriots stood fast behind the barricade and defeated the attacking British, ultimately resulting in the opening of a supply line, via the Chesapeake Bay, to Washington's troops. The course of history could have changed in this one minute had the British won this battle on December 9, 1775.

KAREN TROUTMAN
Alexandria, Virginia

The Beauty Beneath the Surface

Beauty isn't only skin deep. The beautiful caverns containing stalagmites, stalactites, and limestone curtains found in Virginia are proof. The wide variety of formations, colors, and textures of the rocks as well as the crystal-clear underground lakes that can be found deep beneath the surface are remarkable.

KAREN TROUTMAN
Alexandria, Virginia

Piecing Together Life in the New World at Jamestown

This scene depicts the *Susan Constant* at the Jamestown Colony landing. Colonists braved the unknown to come to the New World at Jamestown with just what they could carry on the ship. One of the cabin boys on the first ships, James Brumfield, was a very distant relative of mine.

KAREN TROUTMAN
Alexandria, Virginia

Soaring over the Shenandoah Valley

The Shenandoah Valley and the Blue Ridge Mountains have been the scene for much of Virginia's history, native life, colonists' exploration, battles, agriculture, and recreation. Often, hot-air balloons can be seen exploring the area from the heights. These balloon rides allow adventurous souls the opportunity to experience the breathtaking scenery from an unforgettable perspective.

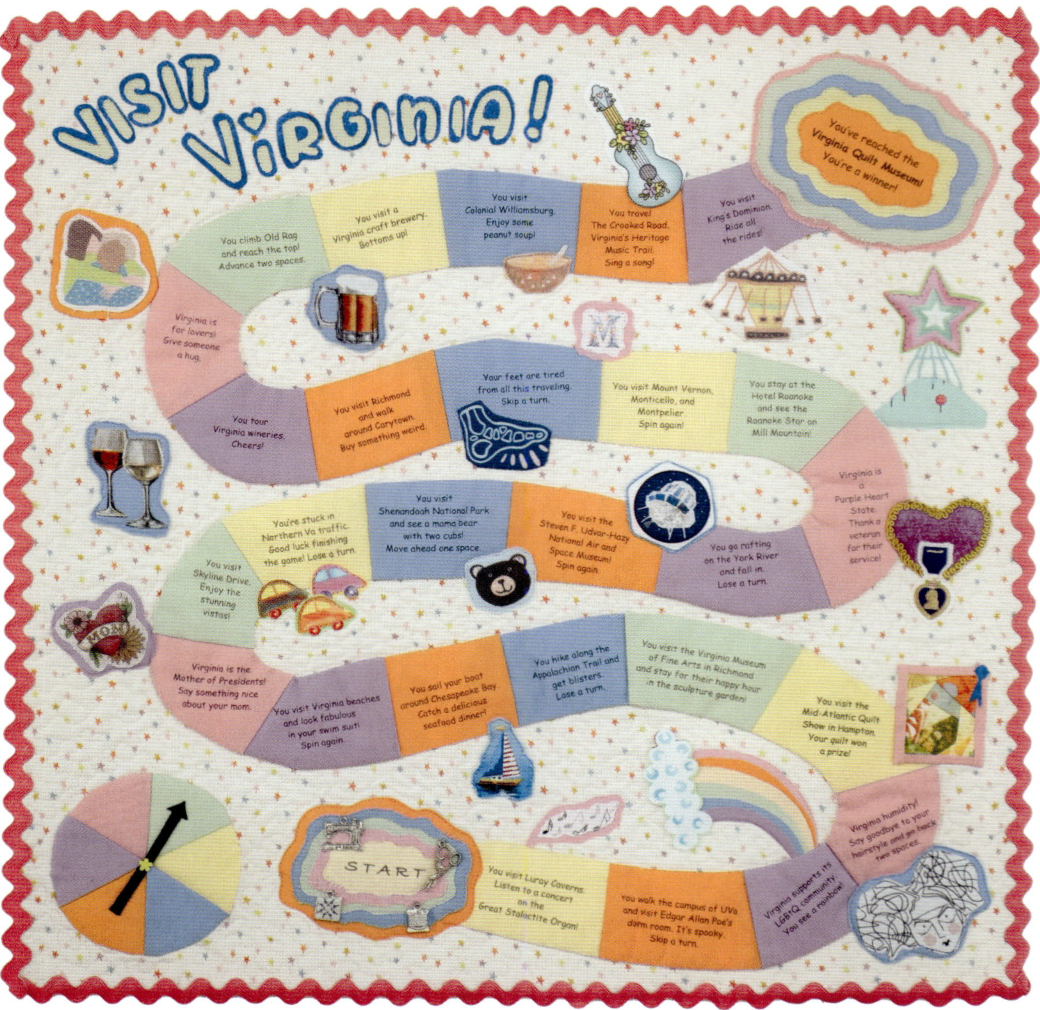

MAGGIE WARD

Warrenton, Virginia

Visit Virginia

Tourism is a vital part of Virginia's economy. Pick your token, spin the dial, and head out on a road trip through Virginia's points of interest. With this game board quilt, I hope to remind Virginians that we have a wide variety of historical, geological, and cultural elements at our doorstep just waiting to be experienced.

PAT WASHBURN
Chantilly, Virginia

Cabell's Mill

Cabell's Mill was originally constructed as a gristmill in the eighteenth century. It provided mill services for the community and later evolved to be an essential community gathering space. Today it and its surrounding gardens provide a beautiful place for the Fairfax County community to gather and celebrate special occasions. The mill is situated in the lovely Ellanor C. Lawrence Park in Centerville.

M. CHRISTINE WATSON
Richmond, Virginia

Ebb and Flow

The salt marshes and estuaries of the Chesapeake Bay have been vital to Virginia's history, offering environmental, cultural, and economic benefits. Acting as natural buffers, they protect coastal areas from flooding and erosion, supporting agriculture and coastal communities. Their role in filtering pollutants and improving water quality is essential for the health of the bay. Today, conserving these ecosystems is crucial for protecting against climate change, rising sea levels, and environmental degradation, ensuring their ongoing importance to Virginia's history and future.

Tapestry of Bay Fishes

The fish of Chesapeake Bay have shaped Virginia's history, economy, culture, and environment. Once vital for survival and trade, fish remain important today. Overfishing has led to conservation efforts, while fishing regulations influence Virginia's policies.

KAREN WEST
Union Hall, Virginia

Smith Mountain Lake

Smith Mountain Lake is a large man-made lake in southwestern Virginia. The lake was created in the 1960s by building a dam in the gap at Smith Mountain, in Bedford and Pittsylvania Counties. Two rivers, the Roanoke and the Blackwater, converge to form the lake. The dam is a hydroelectric power plant built and owned by American Electric Power (AEP). The electricity produced provides power during peak periods over the large AEP system. The lake was filled to capacity in 1966. With 20,000 acres and 500 miles of shoreline, the lake has become a very popular recreation spot for boaters and swimmers and is considered one of the jewels of southwestern Virginia. The Blue Ridge Mountain backdrop, unforgettable views, picturesque skies, and diverse fishing and wildlife make it a key destination for water-loving residents and vacationers.

BETH WIESNER

Woodbridge, Virginia

Pumpkin Love

This quilt represents nature and farming in Prince William County. The Doeg Indigenous people's primary camp was located on the north bank of the Occoquan River, where they raised pumpkins, among other crops, so it seemed fitting to tie the two together. A cardinal was a natural for the bird block, and while the refuge is known primarily for its migratory birds, some visit to see the wildflowers. The Occoquan Bay National Wildlife Refuge is a quiet area of Prince William County with an important history.

ROSANNE WILLIAMSON

Warrenton, Virginia

Fauquier County Historic Court House

This stately historic building was rebuilt in 1890 after fire destroyed three other structures on the same site. The building currently houses the County General District Court of the 20th Judicial District. During the Civil War, Warrenton experienced alternating bouts of occupation by both the Union and Confederate troops. Col. John S. Mosby, known as the "Gray Ghost," made Warrenton part of his focus during the war and his home after the conflict. A monument to him is in the courthouse yard.

ROSANNE WILLIAMSON

Warrenton, Virginia

Graffiti House

The Graffiti House is a two-story frame structure built at the intersection of two railroad tracks that, in the mid-nineteenth century, connected points north with much of the rest of Virginia. While the outside of the house looks quite ordinary, the walls inside contain a treasure of charcoal and pencil drawings and signatures left by soldiers from both armies during the Civil War. The Graffiti House was purchased by the Brandy Station Foundation in 2002.

KATY WOMACK
Woodstock, Virginia

Camp Roosevelt

President Franklin D. Roosevelt promised a "New Deal" to put the nation back to work. The Civilian Conservation Corps (CCC) was launched in the Virginia Blue Ridge Mountains on April 17, 1933, in what is now George Washington National Forest. This camp was named Camp Roosevelt and was the first established CCC camp in Virginia and in America. By the end of 1935, there were over 2,650 camps operating, and enrollees performed more than one hundred kinds of work. The CCC had great public support, and the young, inexperienced labor force exceeded all expectations. The men earned $30 per month, of which $25 was sent home to their families. Nationwide, eight hundred state parks were built, leaving a lasting legacy for others to enjoy. The enrollees' contributions to our nation have endured.

KEVIN WOMACK
Forest, Virginia

Aquia Sandstone

This piece is an abstract showing the beauty of this stone that was so important in shaping the buildings of our young nation. Located nearly 40 miles south of Washington, DC, this sandstone quarry is in the woods of Stafford County. Stone from it was used on the exterior wall of the White House and on homes of numerous prominent eighteenth-century Virginians.

CHAPTER 2

Unfinished Revolutions

In 1776, the Second Continental Congress signed the Declaration of Independence, stating in the preamble, "We hold these truths to be self-evident, that all men are created equal, that they are endowed by their Creator with certain unalienable Rights, that among these are Life, Liberty and the pursuit of Happiness."

Since then, the United States has grappled with fulfilling that promise. With the theme "Unfinished Revolutions," we encouraged quilters to examine the different fights for life, liberty, and the pursuit of happiness that have occurred and still are occurring.

Our quilters shared works that showcased slavery, the suffrage movement of the late 1800s and early 1900s, the civil rights movement of the 1960s, the fight for LGBTQA+ rights today, and numerous other unfinished revolutions throughout our history. Many of these national movements included people, places, and events that happened in or are related to Virginia. These struggles are not linear movements; there are setbacks and pauses in all revolutions, and many of these ideas are still works in progress today.

This *Fish Crazy Quilt* is a unique textile that embodies the thought that there are unfinished aspects of our history. This crazy patchwork in the form of a fish is made up of ⅞-inch squares, with embroidered feather stitches surrounding each square. The remainder of the design is filled with patches and embroidery stitches around all stars and fans, which are appliquéd.

Lucinda Robinson-Rice created this piece in the 1880s. She was from the Endless Caverns area in Virginia but moved with her family by covered wagon to settle in Illinois at age five. She would later visit relatives in Virginia, where she met her husband, Dr. Francis Eugene Rice. She then moved to New Market, Virginia. This quilt was often pulled out by Lucinda's great-grandchildren on rainy days, and they would look at the embroidery on the quilt.

Fish Crazy Quilt, Lucinda Robinson-Rice, New Market, Virginia, 26" × 52", circa 1885. Collection of the Virginia Quilt Museum.

NANCY B. ADAMS
Annandale, Virginia

April 16, 2007

This piece commemorates the mass shooting that occurred at Virginia Tech when an undergraduate student killed thirty-two people and wounded seventeen others with two semiautomatic pistols. This event called attention to a review of gun laws and gaps in mental health care.

MONA B. ALDERSON
Mountain City, Tennessee

Vigilant: The Intelligence Community in Northern Virginia

This piece depicts the intelligence community's presence in Northern Virginia and its significant role in the defense of the nation in conducting activities necessary in foreign relations and the protection of the national security of the US. The outline of Virginia forms the base of the design, with a pentagon shape and a compass as other focal points. The compass rose is a primary feature of the seal of the Central Intelligence Agency; there is a pentagon, since nine intelligence community organizations are part of the Department of Defense, including the National Reconnaissance Office and the National Geospatial-Intelligence Agency, both headquartered in Northern Virginia. Both the Office of the Director of National Intelligence—the head of the intelligence community—and the CIA are independent agencies with headquarters in McLean, Virginia. Men and women of the intelligence community, who remain vigilant for all of us, are largely unknown and unrecognized. We cannot take our freedoms for granted and must remain watchful against those who would take them away.

DIANA ANGLERO
Stephens City, Virginia

Maggie Lena Walker

Maggie Lena Walker was an outstanding Black businesswoman who is better known as the first Black American woman who was the founder and president of a bank. Walker was also a civil rights activist. She led by example and became the best-known African American woman in Virginia in the early 1900s, nationally recognized as an advocate for women, children, and education.

LISA ARTHAUD
Warrenton, Virginia

Ticked Off

Under section 29.1-521 of the Virginia Code, it is illegal to hunt or kill any animal, even a "nuisance" animal and even on private land, on Sundays, a rest day for all species of wild bird and wild animal life, except raccoons, which may be hunted until 2:00 a.m. on Sundays. The law was amended in 2022 to allow Sunday hunting for all land game species, without raccoon prejudice.

ANNE AUBRY
Front Royal, Virginia

In Defense of Books, Libraries, and Librarians

The Samuels Public Library, or the Front Royal Librarian Society, as it was known at its inception, was the second subscription public library in the commonwealth of Virginia. It was chartered in 1799 in Front Royal to foster literacy and provide access to books in the Shenandoah Valley. This piece represents the street front of the current library building, which opened in June 2009. As schools and public libraries face book bans, censorship, and threats to funding, I want this quilt to remind viewers of the important role that libraries play in communities, in the hope that librarians will continue to have the freedom of selecting books on the basis of the needs of all their readers, and not on the political agenda of a few.

GINGER BROTHERS
Huddleston, Virginia

In Our Hands

On Sunday, November 12, 2023, a fire broke out in a remote corner where the Blue Ridge Parkway and George Washington and Thomas Jefferson National Forests all meet. This view of the Matt's Creek fire was inspired by the view from the northern edge of Bedford County. For a week, residents had to take extreme caution as smoke from the blaze became increasingly hazardous. While the cause of the fire is listed as unknown, on the basis of the location, many experts and officials suspect that the spark of a cigarette butt was the root cause. The wrist of the hand shown is tattooed with a number: 11,020. This is the number of acres lost to this one wildfire, which lasted for only four days. Due to the size of our forests, Virginians are dependent on one another to adhere to wildfire prevention rules. This impacts the forest industry, which is the second-largest industry in Virginia. During the time it took to create this piece, nearly 3,000 more acres were lost to wildfires in Virginia. We must pay attention to the causes and prevention of wildfires; if we don't, not only will our iconic forests and wildlife be at risk, but also lives of Virginians.

JEAN CARIDEO
Chesapeake, Virginia

Contradictions

The enslavement of Black men, women, and children in Revolutionary-era Virginia posed a major contradiction to the ideals of freedom and independence from English rule. Thomas Jefferson, George Washington, James Monroe, and James Madison all were wealthy eighteenth-century farmers . . . and slave owners. Since enslaved people were critical to the economies of the Southern colonies, they chose to skirt the issue of enslavement in order to unify all the colonies against Britain. They also believed that there would never be an "America" if they challenged the institution of colonial slavery. Because England controlled the production of cloth and restricted the colonies from access to mechanized cloth production, most quilts found in colonial Virginia were made abroad. Fine cottons, silks, calamancos, and linens were the fabrics of the well-to-do. Coarse wools, homespun, and rough weaves were for the poor and enslaved. Thomas Jefferson would have had a silk quilt produced by professional quilters in England, while his enslaved would have had quilts made of cheaper fabrics he chose to give them. Contradictions are part of the fabric that makes us human. Until the contradictions of racial inequality are solved, there will never be freedom and justice for all in America.

JEAN CARIDEO
Chesapeake, Virginia

Separate . . . but Equal?

Cornland School was a one-room schoolhouse in Norfolk County (now the city of Chesapeake), Virginia, established for the education of Black children during Virginia's segregated "separate but equal" period. Cornland operated from 1903 until 1952, when the Norfolk Country School Board recognized that building a new school consolidating the country's schools for Black children was cheaper than the lawsuits they foresaw from the strong possibility of upcoming federal desegregation laws. Cornland is one of the region's earliest Reconstruction-era efforts at formalized education for African American students. Built and funded mostly by families of students and other members of the Cornland community, it is a testament not only to the unequal conditions of schools, but also to the perseverance, pride, sacrifice, and reverence for education that made this school "a safe place in an unsafe world" for so many of its students. Segregation in the schools was a reality that needs to be recognized. Ignoring, canceling, or trivializing this history will not result in the promise of America to establish equality for all its citizens.

T CARTER
Alexandria, Virginia

Finally Federally Recognized: Indigenous Nations of the Chesapeake Bay Watershed

The Pamunkey became the first tribe in Virginia to be granted federal recognition in 2016. In 2018, an act of Congress recognized the Chickahominy, Eastern Chickahominy, Upper Mattaponi, Rappahannock, Monacan, and Nansemond as sovereign nations. It took over four hundred years to recognize the people who welcomed the first colonists to their shores!

Tauxenent/Doeg: The Land Has Memory

It's important to acknowledge that the land now called the commonwealth of Virginia was inhabited and thriving long before the English colonists arrived. The Doeg people lived in a prominent town called Tauxenent, located in present-day Northern Virginia, along the Occoquan River. The Virginia militia led an extermination campaign against them and seized their ancestral lands in the late seventeenth century. Doeg survivors converged with Pamunkey, Rappahannock, Piscataway, and other local tribes. Although they did not survive as a nation, they are still here.

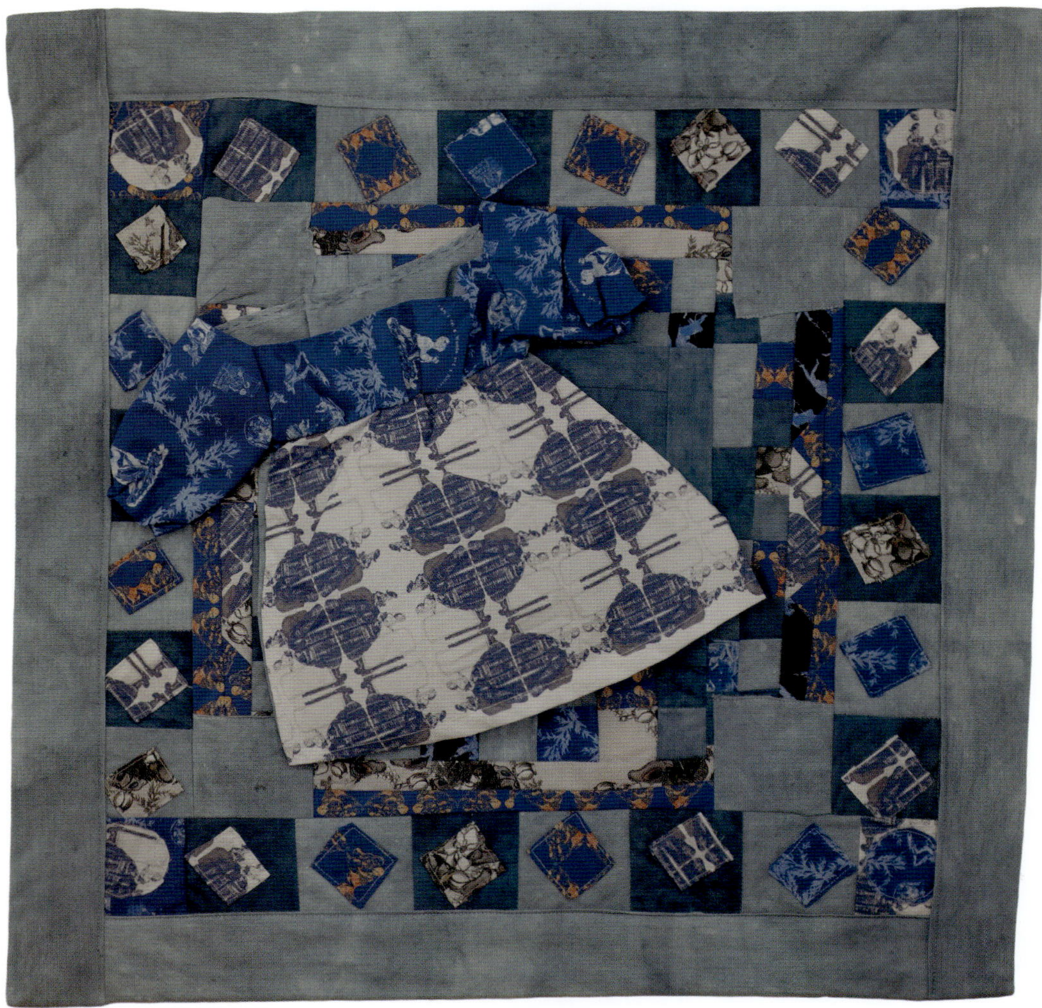

CAROLINE CREEDEN

Ellicott City, Maryland

Women, Martha, and Slavery

This piece, based on Martha Washington's Children's Game quilt, depicts women as influential in racial dynamics rather as innocent bystanders. Martha's granddaughters preserved fragments of her clothing, inspiring my use of fragments. A doll's dress represents how women taught their children racial superiority and trained them as mistresses of the house. Clothing was passed down between women, as were social viewpoints and beliefs. Children observed actions of adults. The fabric designs show white women in positions of power. Representing the role that women played in slavery/racial hierarchy is important, since men are often presented as the abusers and women as innocent. Many Virginia women, both wealthy and poor, participated in slavery by owning and selling people, witnessing or participating in acts of violence without remorse, and holding white nationalist viewpoints. Martha's views on slavery never changed, although her husband's did. Too often it is forgotten or dismissed, because of the perception that women were ignorant or too genteel to understand what was really happening. But many women who owned enslaved persons understood the act of bondage and the financial benefits it brought to their purse, and their disregard of morals.

POLLY DAVIS
Warrenton, Virginia

Dancing for Change

The protests that gained traction in the summer of 2020 and still continue were countrywide and drew a wide variety of people. In the wake of multiple Black lives being taken without just cause, at the hands of those meant to uphold the law, the protests drew attention to the disparate (and often fatal) punishment being meted out to people of color. The protests in Richmond, at the base of monuments honoring Confederate officers, resulted in the long-overdue removal of some of the offensive statues and removal of their names from buildings and streets, not just in Richmond but in other cities as well. The fight for equal justice continues.

ROBERTA DEWEES
Springfield, Virginia

Donkey Bathing in Culpeper

Did you know that in Culpeper, Virginia, it is illegal to bathe a donkey on the sidewalk? We really don't know the reason why this law was written, but some think it is a leftover of our founding fathers' blue laws. Blue laws, also known as Sunday laws, were created to regulate Sunday activities when people were expected to attend church services and observe Sunday as a day of rest. There are many funny laws regarding donkey bathing around the country. The interesting question is this: What must have happened to necessitate such a law in Culpeper? According to "The Lawyer Portal," in the 1920s a home in Arizona was flooded while a donkey was asleep in a bathtub. Eventually the tub filled up and flooded, and the animal was swept away. The townspeople were able to rescue the poor animal, but the event resulted soon after in a law intended to avoid such an occurrence from happening again.

EILEEN DOUGHTY
Vienna, Virginia

History Lesson

With a modification of the traditional School House block, this quilt tells the story of Virginia's slow move from segregated public schools (black and white fabrics), to the shameful era of Massive Resistance, to the vibrancy and welcoming integrated atmosphere of today (colorful fabrics). The center building shown is Louise Archer Elementary School, the last in Fairfax County to be desegregated, which today contains a wonderful mix of cultures and languages in the student body.

SUSAN PRICE
Springfield, Virginia

Loving v. Virginia

Loving v. Virginia was the 1967 US Supreme Court case that ruled that laws banning interracial marriage violate the Equal Protection and Due Process Clauses of the Fourteenth Amendment to the US Constitution. Because of this landmark civil rights decision, I have had the privilege to celebrate my interracial marriage since 1976.

GAYLE FERRELL
Midland, Virginia

Airlie Waterfall—Birthplace of Earth Day

Here is the iconic and often-photographed waterfall on the grounds of the Airlie Conference Center—popularly called "Airlie" in Warrenton, Virginia. The birth of the idea behind Earth Day, celebrated globally each April 22, began at Airlie in November 1969, when Wisconsin senator Gaylord Nelson and California representative Pete McCloskey spoke to a group of medical and law students there. The presence of a *New York Times* reporter contributed to Nelson's and McCloskey's words getting national attention. The idea became a reality the following year, when the first Earth Day was celebrated by millions of Americans holding rallies, marches, and teach-ins, with the goal of making people more aware of environmental protection. The celebration of Earth Day is vitally important for all planet inhabitants, just as it was when it began in 1970, and is currently observed only in the United States.

SHEILA RIESS
Ellicott City, Maryland

Winchester, Virginia

Winchester is known as the "apple capital." Vast orchards here form the largest apple-producing area in all of Virginia, and it is the site of the largest apple export market in the nation. Winchester, a beautiful small town, has hosted for nearly one hundred years the popular annual Shenandoah Apple Blossom Festival.

PRISCILLA GODFREY
Philomont, Virginia

Loudoun County Cows vs. Dulles Airport

The construction of Dulles Airport in Northern Virginia drastically changed Loudoun County from a rural area to a suburban area. The airport brought water and septic facilities to a county that was previously well and septic field drainage. In the 1940s, Loudoun County was number one for milk production. Now it has only two dairies, the Brookfield Dairy and the Dogwood Farm. Before the airport was built, nearby Sterling, Virginia, was rural, and farms covered most of its land. The airport made that property valuable to developers, and farms were replaced by houses.

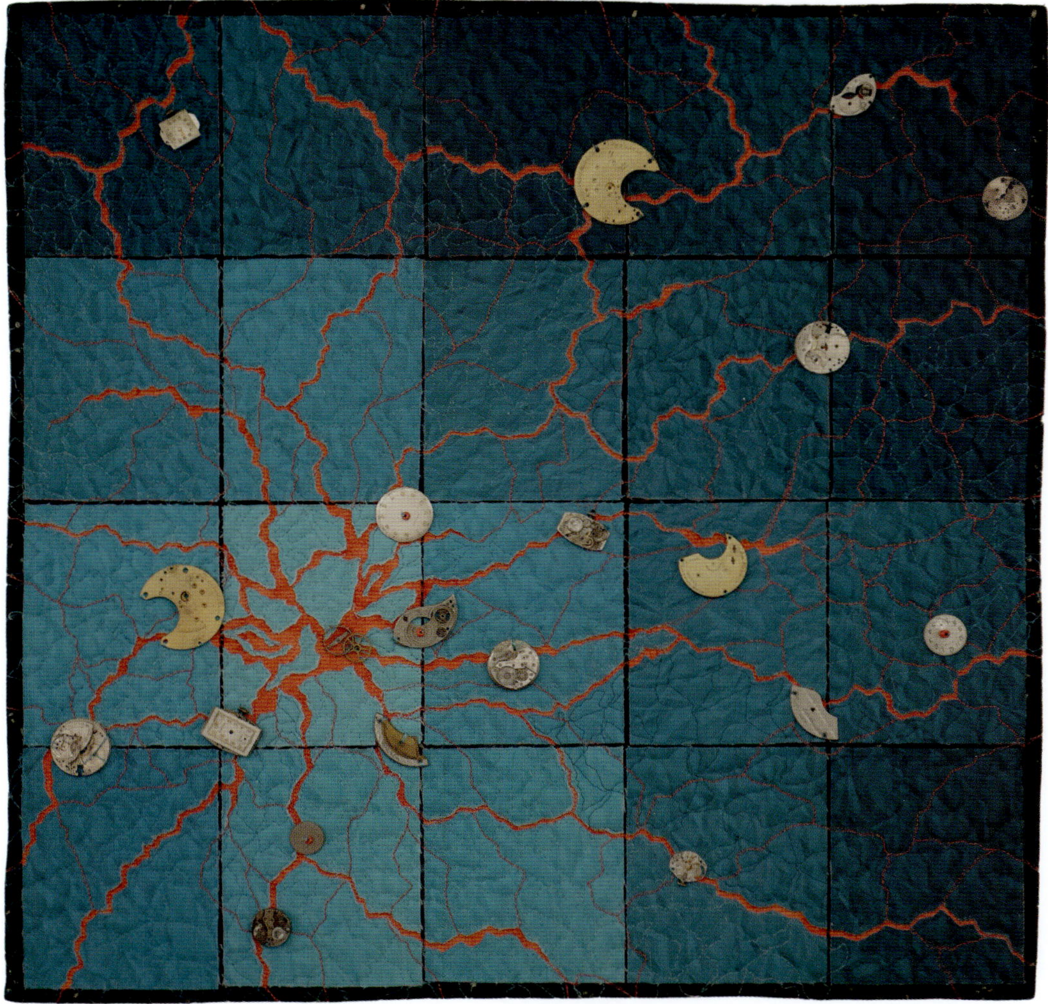

ROBIN HAMILL
Charlottesville, Virginia

Broken Times

The serial numbers on these antique watch pieces were traced to events that are often ignored because they show a darker side of Virginia's past. Examples I researched to depict include the following: Virginia's secession from the Union in 1861; the Civil War, which led to the deaths of 32,751 Virginians, the most of any state; a year during the post–Civil War Reconstruction period, 1867, which was fraught with poverty and racial violence; the passage of the Mapp Act in 1916, leading to a burgeoning moonshine business brought about by Prohibition; the year that KKK membership in Virginia reached its peak, in 1923; the 1927 *Buck v. Bell* US Supreme Court case, which legalized forced sterilization of "inferiors" and was in place until the 1970s (Carrie Buck was a resident of Albemarle County who became pregnant following a rape; she was of average intelligence, not an "imbecile," as the case purports); about 66 percent of public schools in Virginia closing to control costs in 1932, as a result of the Depression; and, in 1933, Hitler coming to power and passing statutes that were based on the principles expressed in *Buck v. Bell*—for example, the Nazis learned to do tubal ligations at the Lynchburg School. Not all history is glowing.

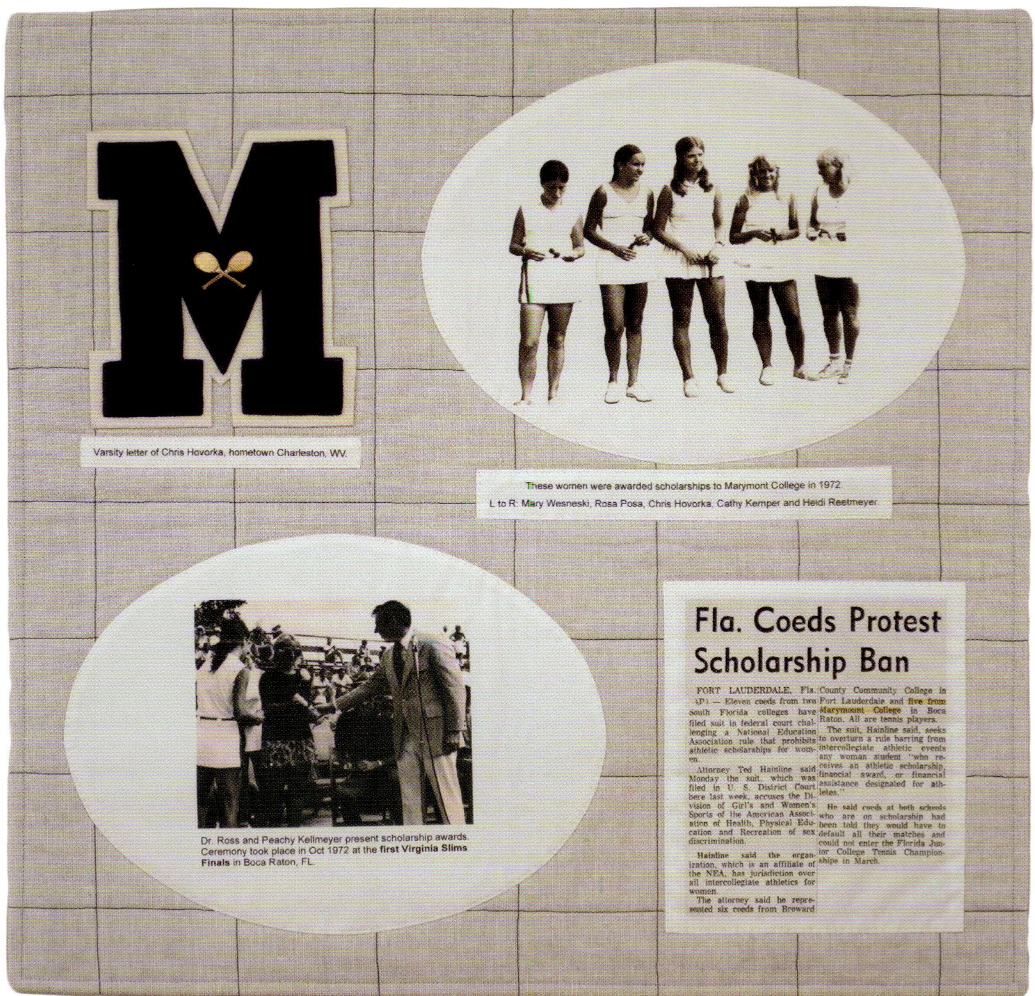

Fla. Coeds Protest Scholarship Ban

FORT LAUDERDALE, Fla. (AP) — Eleven coeds from two South Florida colleges have filed suit in federal court challenging a National Education Association rule that prohibits athletic scholarships for women.

Attorney Ted Hainline said Monday the suit, which was filed in U. S. District Court here last week, accuses the Division of Girl's and Women's Sports of the American Association of Health, Physical Education and Recreation of sex discrimination.

Hainline said the organization, which is an affiliate of the NEA, has jurisdiction over all intercollegiate athletics for women.

The attorney said he represented six coeds from Broward County Community College in Fort Lauderdale and five from Marymount College in Boca Raton. All are tennis players.

The suit, Hainline said, seeks to overturn a rule barring from intercollegiate athletic events any woman student "who receives an athletic scholarship, financial award, or financial assistance designated for athletes."

He said coeds at both schools who are on scholarship had been told they would have to default all their matches and could not enter the Florida Junior College Tennis Championships in March.

HEIDI HAYNES
Winchester, Virginia

Kellmeyer and Scholarships for Women

Title IX of the Civil Rights Act became law in June 1972. That same year, Marymount College offered tennis scholarships to five women. The physical education director was Fern Lee "Peachy" Kellmeyer, and one of those players was Chris Hovorka, both native West Virginians. At that time, women's athletics were governed by the Association for Interscholastic Athletics for Women (AIAW). AIAW had an anti-athletic scholarship policy based on long-held beliefs that commercializing women's competitions would make women do "unwomanly things." Players were denied entry into the AIAW championship competition, and scholarship recipients had to default all matches. Kellmeyer, along with these students, challenged the AIAW's antischolarship policy on the grounds that it violated the Fourteenth amendment and Title IX. The Kellmeyer-initiated lawsuit caused an AIAW rule change to allow women to receive athletic scholarships, and it revolutionized women's athletics. The challenge to the inequality of the rules has had a significant impact in supporting women athletes for over fifty years, but inequalities remain to this day, and gains are still being challenged. In 2011, Kellmeyer was inducted into the International Tennis Hall of Fame.

MARY KERR
Woodbridge, Virginia

Votes for Women

The US suffrage movement was a long and difficult battle. The first women's-rights convention was held in July 1848, and for the next seventy years, activists fought to make their voices heard. American women did not receive the right to vote until 1920, with the ratification of the Nineteenth Amendment to the US Constitution. One of the darkest moments of this era was when protesters were jailed and tortured at the Occoquan Workhouse in Lorton, Virginia. This quilt depicts brave women who proudly carried the Votes for Women banner. The silhouettes are marching across a vintage crazy quilt that is dated 1897.

KIMBERLY MORROW LEONG
Fairfax, Virginia

Suburban Harvest

The *Loving v. Virginia* case, decided by the Supreme Court in 1967, struck down existing laws forbidding interracial marriages and ruled them unconstitutional. This piece depicts a biracial child living an uneventful suburban life in Manassas with her white mother and Chinese father. The utterly ordinary act of harvesting the first onion from the family's garden in the yard of a newly built townhouse in the mid-1990s exemplifies the profound changes that *Loving v. Virginia* brought to Virginia. Normalizing the blending of cultures and families is also a symbol of the changes that were already underway in Northern Virginia, since it was growing as a technology center and was soon to be a destination for people from all around the world. The current political climate, with charged conversations about race and immigration across the state and country, tells us that conversations about race are unfinished. This piece is a snapshot of what has been, what is, and what could be.

DORA LOCKWOOD
Fairfax Station, Virginia

SOPHEA TOUCH
Fairfax, Virginia

From Darkness Comes Unity

At the end of the American Civil War, General Robert E. Lee emerged as one of the leading advocates for peace, restoration, and national unity. Although he personally opposed slavery on a philosophical level, he supported its legality and held hundreds of enslaved persons throughout his life. When Virginia seceded from the Union in 1861, Lee chose to fight for his home state, despite his conflicted views on slavery. He went on to command the Army of Northern Virginia, the Confederacy's most powerful army. After his surrender to Union general Ulysses S. Grant at Appomattox on April 9, 1865, Lee shifted focus from warfare to healing the nation's wounds. He urged fellow Virginians and former Confederate soldiers to lay down their arms and work toward unity and reconciliation with the North. The quote on this quilt is taken from one of Lee's letters to a former soldier. It emphasizes the importance of moving beyond the darkness of a divided country to rebuilding a unified nation.

SALLY MAXWELL
Poquoson, Virginia

Apollo and Poseidon: Reflections of Poquoson

If you had lived in Poquoson during my mother's childhood, you were either a farmer and worked the land (a "hayseed") or a waterman and worked on the water (a "muddytoe"). In the 1960s, during my childhood, that began to change, and a third employer brought new residents to the city: NASA and the Langley Research Center (LaRC). Virginia played an important part early in the space race, and in 1965, LaRC completed the gantry used to practice landings on a lunar-like surface for the Apollo program. That gantry is across the creek and within sight of my mother's childhood home. Farming is no longer an important part of our community, but watermen still tend crab pots along the tributaries of the Chesapeake Bay. They provide an interesting counterpoint to the structures looking skyward, which are also part of Virginia's heritage.

VIRGINIA MCCONNELL
Manakin Sabot, Virginia

Phoenix

In July 2020, racial protests against the murder of George Floyd turned violent in Richmond. Local businesses were looted and burned, and Confederate monuments were defaced. As the summer progressed, the graffiti on the monuments became increasingly dense with profanity, slogans denouncing the police, and expressions of fury against racism. Mixed in with these cries of rage, however, were messages urging peace and solidarity. As the summer progressed, the Lee monument became a community gathering place. Activists of all racial identities posed in front of the statue, ballerinas danced on its base, families shared picnics on the grass, a basketball hoop was erected. In October, the *New York Times* named the Lee monument as the most influential form of protest art since World War II. From the ashes of its shameful past rises a phoenix, burning with rage, covered in the painted shouts of a people. Glowing with the thousand colors of a new way forward, the monument became a vibrant, colorful community phoenix.

KATHERINE MCPHERSON
Fairfax Station, Virginia

Bull Run to Appomattox

The American Civil War was fought over four years between the Union and the Confederacy. During that time, over 624,000 people died, more from Virginia than any other state. Virginia was the location of the start of the war, it was the Confederate capital, and it is where General Lee surrendered, which led to the end of the war. Most of the men who fought in this war were under the age of twenty-five. They used whatever weapons they could find, and dressed in what they had. The silhouettes in this quilt represent these brave men. The depicted map shows the battles fought in Virginia as researched through the Library of Congress maps. Each knot represents a battle location, and the stars represent the locations of the start and end of the war. About 43 percent of the battles of the war were fought in the commonwealth of Virginia.

CARLY MUL
Hamilton, Virginia

The Battlegrounds of Virginia

This is a visual representation of the fights between the armies of the North and the South. Many of these intense battles took place in Virginia. Long before I ever knew I would be living in the US, my first knowledge of US history came from the TV series *North and South,* in which two friends from West Point became leaders in the opposite armies. It was during the 1980s that I saw this series in the Netherlands. American history is not part of the Dutch high school or college curriculum, and the names of different states, the map, slavery, antebellum houses, plantations, and, yes, even cotton production were all new to me. We moved to the US in 1994, and since 2002 Virginia has been my home. As a quilter, to collage different fabrics together to portray Virginia and the places of famous battlegrounds, the generals "from the TV series," and my current residence takes me full circle.

GENE OLIVER
Martinsburg, West Virginia

The Battle of Falling Waters

The embroidered centerpiece reflects a print published in the July 27, 1861, edition of *Harper's Weekly*. It depicts soldiers of a Wisconsin regiment advancing down the Martinsburg Turnpike (Rt. 11) toward the Porterfield farmhouse. The blocks are Civil War–era patterns that would have been used during that time period. The Battle of Falling Waters (recently officially designated the Battle of Hoke's Run by the National Park Service) occurred on July 2, 1861, outside Martinsburg, West Virginia. After this early battle of the Civil War, participants on both sides would go on to gain fame during the conflict.

CHRISTINE PAYNE

Sterling, Virginia

Patrick Henry: In His Own Words

Patrick Henry was a Virginia orator and lawyer known for eloquent speeches, the most famous of which was his "Give me liberty, or give me death!" address to the Second Virginia Convention in 1775. With his gift of oratory, a sharp mind, and folksy demeanor, he endeared himself to Virginians. He could stir up enthusiasm for colonial causes with fiery speeches and became an admired statesman and friend to Washington, Jefferson, and other colonial leaders of our country. Patrick Henry was Virginia's first governor, and he was encouraged to run for president after Washington declined a third term. He had such a fine reputation within the new government that he was offered several high-ranking positions, but he refused all of them, so that he could go back to his family in Virginia and resume his law practice. A statue of Patrick Henry stands on the grounds of the Virginia Capitol in Richmond among other Virginia founding fathers. A muse beneath his feet represents "Revolution." It is said that his "Give me liberty, or give me death" speech inspired revolutionary action.

LIZ RICH
Rockingham, Virginia

Love Wins

Two major Supreme Court cases relating to marriage equality originated in Virginia. The legalization of interracial marriage and the legalization of same-sex marriage were major civil rights victories for marginalized groups. Commemorating these events is important because it adds voices to history that are otherwise silenced. Virginia history cannot truly be represented if the histories of marginalized groups are left out.

LUANA RUBIN
Boulder, Colorado

Enslaved People of Mount Vernon

Nearly six hundred slaves built and maintained George Washington's household and plantation at Mount Vernon. If you have a chance to visit the historic site, you can take a tour, visit the slave quarters, and learn more about the enslaved. The story of our founding fathers and the reality of who physically built our country is complicated. Although George Washington employed slaves, later in life he was antislavery, stipulating in his will that slaves employed at Mount Vernon would be granted freedom after his wife's death. In 1983 a memorial was built on the property to honor the enslaved.

RICKI SELVA
Gig Harbor, Washington

James Madison

James Madison, our fourth president, from 1809 to 1817, is often called the "Father of the Constitution." The main authors of the Federalist Papers and, by extension, the US Constitution, were James Madison, Alexander Hamilton, and John Jay. At the Constitutional Convention, Madison advocated for constitutional principles of separation of powers, checks and balances, bicameralism, and federalism. Madison wrote the first ten amendments as a solution to limit government power and protect individual liberties through the Constitution. Madison held contradictory views on slavery throughout his life, arguing that slavery was incompatible with Revolutionary principles even as he owned over one hundred enslaved persons on his Virginia plantation, brought enslaved people to the White House, and ultimately sold them for personal profit.

SHERYL SIMS

Alexandria, Virginia

Madonna of the Trails

The Madonna of the Trail monuments are twelve identical statues commissioned in the states where the National Old Trails Road passed. They provide a symbol of the strength, determination, and courage in the midst of bravely conquering the wilderness and creating homes for their families. The National Society of the Daughters of the American Revolution commissioned sculptor August Leimbach to create the statues, one of which is in Wheeling, West Virginia. Women have always demonstrated strength, courage, and love in supporting the people and things they care about, many times without getting the credit they deserve. These monuments pay tribute to their determination, intellect, and adaptability in having the ability to conquer the wilderness.

SHERYL SIMS
Alexandria, Virginia

Union Jail

Union Jail has a sad history for housing enslaved persons as well as prisoners during both the Revolutionary War and the Civil War. Originally built in 1812 as a residence, in 1828 the property became a huge jail complex for slaves, where thousands of African men, women, and children were bought and sold. The property was so large that it took up half of a city block. It was located in historic Alexandria at 1315 Duke Street. At last, upon liberation in 1861, thanks to Lincoln and the Northern army, the city of Alexandria became a safe haven for African Americans. Eventually purchased by the city, the renovated Freedom House Museum that remains is a significant reminder of the past when we try to understand the past, present, and history of matters of race and equity.

PRISCILLA STULTZ
Williamsburg, Virginia

Homelessness: No Place to Call Home

The homeless have always been with us; sadly, homelessness is on the rise in Virginia. For every 10,000 people living in the state, 7.8 are homeless. Most of the time we ignore their existence, and no one wants someone camping out in their neighborhood. There is a place called House of Mercy in my area. Local churches contribute time, money, and food for those less fortunate, but still there are so many. So many are veterans who fought to sustain our freedom but have lost their way. My heart weeps whenever I hear their stories. Veterans Affairs tries to help, but without more money and efforts, the veteran can fall through the cracks in society. The homeless single mother, the runaway, the immigrant, the veteran, and the uneducated all need help. We need to do more—maybe this quilt will open someone's eyes.

KATHRYN TEAGUE
Burke, Virginia

Virginia: Before, Birth, Now, Next

Virginia has not treated all citizens equally over time. Much progress has been made, but we are still finding new ways to prevent equal access, and we tend to focus on differences rather than commonalities. Recently, it seems like we have forgotten the struggles we overcame and the progress we made, and we are again focused on what divides us. Yet if we come together now, we all can prosper. In this abstract piece, fabric patterns and colors were selected to represent what is described for each quadrant. The Before panel (*bottom left*) shows Indigenous inhabitants and the slave trade. The Birth panel (*top left*) depicts wars, violence, and enslavement of people, and the taking of land for statehood. The Now panel (*bottom right*) highlights the evolution of modern Virginia—the Great Migration, busing to integrate, *Loving v. Virginia*, political gerrymandering, segregation of bathrooms by race and for transgender people, balance between urbanization and nature, and more. The Next panel (*top right*) shows a hopeful future—Virginians living in unity and in harmony with nature. All panels have bright red for war, violence, and death, except for the Next panel, where red hearts represent the hope that we can live united as We the People.

BETSY TRUE
Alexandria, Virginia

Mary Smith Peake and the Emancipation Oak

Mary Smith Peake (1823–1862) was an extraordinary woman who taught Black enslaved and free people at a time when it was illegal to do so. She started a charity to help the poor and infirm. Her early teaching took place under a live oak tree in Hampton, Virginia, and later in a cottage that became the beginning of Hampton University. After her death, the oak was chosen to be the place where the Emancipation Proclamation was first read to the people of Hampton, becoming known as the Emancipation Oak. That oak still stands today.

KARLA VERNON
Vienna, Virginia

Appomattox

This is the McLean House in Appomattox Court House, Virginia. It is where the signing of documents by Grant and Lee ended the Civil War. The surrender at Appomattox is a bittersweet event because it did not address many of the remaining issues associated with the conflict. While it is a positive event in that it ended a brutal civil war and led to abolishing slavery in the US, more than 150 years after Appomattox the US is still struggling to provide equal rights and equal opportunities to all. In the quilt, the symbolic peace lily climbs up the trellis, into the chimney, and out of the fireplace hearth into the room. Generals Lee and Grant are black stick figures because black is the mixture of all colors. The Confederate and Union flags are depicted on their shoulders in the variations that were correct for 1865.

ARLENE WAGNER
Falls Church, Virginia

Judaism in Virginia

Judaism in the commonwealth of Virginia can be traced back to the 1500s. One significant contribution of Judaism to Virginia was the purchase of Monticello, Thomas Jefferson's estate in Charlottesville. In 1836, Jewish naval captain Uriah P. Levy purchased and restored the estate, ensuring its enduring legacy. Unfortunately, on August 12, 2017, Charlottesville was the site of the Unite the Right Rally, in which white supremacist groups espousing neo-Nazi and white-only ideology gathered, causing the death of three people and injuring at least thirty-five others. Currently there are over fifty synagogues in Virginia. I've contributed this menorah (a symbol of Judaism) quilt to draw attention to positive contributions of Jews in Virginia, and also to call attention to the rise of anti-Semitism due to the rise of the Christian white nationalist movement.

MAGGIE WARD
Warrenton, Virginia

Charlottesville Aftermath

The site of the "Unite the Right" uprising in 2017 was an ominous reminder that our democratic way of life isn't guaranteed. On that day, American-born Nazi sympathizers marched to spread their vitriol through the streets of Charlottesville. When it was over, one woman was dead and many more were injured. The street memorial that sprung up in the wake of the riot was heart-wrenching, reflecting the grief, fear, and anger the community felt at this horror. Clearly the founding fathers' revolution against tyranny didn't end with victory over the British in 1783. It persists today, as we continue the struggle to make "equality for all" a reality.

WILMA GERALD
Norfolk, Virginia

Freedom's Fortress

Freedom's Fortress, also known as Fort Monroe, is where General Benjamin T. Butler decided to accept escaping enslaved persons as "contraband of war." Thousands of formerly enslaved people found sanctuary here. This block depicts my view of the casting off of chains before the bright light of freedom. Fort Monroe earned its place in history for what is known today as the *Contraband* decision. On May 23, 1861, three slaves belonging to Col. Charles Mallory of the Confederate army escaped to the fort. The following day, Mallory's emissary, Maj. John B. Cary, arrived at the fort and demanded that Maj. Gen. Benjamin Butler, the fort's commander, return the runaways in accordance with the Fugitive Slave Act. On May 27, Butler replied that because Virginia now claimed to be a foreign country, this law no longer applied; the three enslaved persons were "contraband of war" and would not be returned to bondage. Word of this decision echoed throughout local Black communities, and within a short time, dozens and then hundreds of enslaved persons sought refuge at Fort Monroe, which they called the "freedom fort." This decision was the first step in the enlistment of thousands of Black men into the Union forces and the issuance of President Abraham Lincoln's Emancipation Proclamation.

CHAPTER 3

Virginia Experiments

Virginia has been home to some great inventions, ideas, and advancements in science, and our quilts provide a wonderful medium in which to celebrate them. Thomas Jefferson invented the swivel chair while at Monticello, Cyrus McCormick patented the mechanical reaper in the Shenandoah Valley, the NASA Langley Research Center has been instrumental in the space race, and Charles Browne Fleet invented ChapStick in Lynchburg. Virginia entrepreneurs were and are instrumental in moving our country forward.

The use of the intricate Pine Burr block is a fabulous example of design innovation in quilting. These blocks are unusual since they are constructed by taking a small square and folding it into a triangle, then sewing one edge to the foundation, therefore layering it against other pieces. There is no interior batting or decorative quilting. Pine Burrs are primarily associated with African American communities in the Southern United States. Pine Burr quilts are also known as Target quilts, Pine Cone quilts, Prairie Points, or Bull's Eye and can be traced to the mid-nineteenth century.

This quilt was donated to the Virginia Quilt Museum by the widow of Gene Spencer, Martha Houle. She recalls that Gene had many vivid memories of sleeping under the quilt (which weighs 24 pounds) as he stayed with his maternal grandmother, "Hattie" Tennessee, in Emporia, Virginia. The family is not sure who made the quilt but attributes it to Hattie.

Pine Burr Quilt, Emporia, Virginia, 90" × 90", circa 1930. Collection of the Virginia Quilt Museum.

DIANA ANGLERO

Stephens City, Virginia

Cheers with Virginia Wines

The practice of wine making in Virginia can be traced back to 1762, and it increased during the 1800s. After many obstacles along the way, such as Prohibition and Virginia's challenging clay-heavy soil, wine making made a comeback and returned to prominence in the 1970s. Grape varieties brought from Europe, together with the native-bred Virginia grape Norton, are now grown by wineries in Virginia. The state is home to nearly three hundred wineries that produce some amazing, award-winning, artisanal wines. These small family businesses contribute significantly to our tourism economy.

LISA ARTHAUD

Warrenton, Virginia

Bonnie's Pony Tale

Bonnie Zacherle, a longtime resident of Warrenton, describes the childhood inspiration for her iconic toy design of My Little Pony: When she was a little girl, her father was stationed in Japan, where she had the opportunity to ride a Korean pack pony named "Nicker." She'd ride and yell out, "This is my little pony." Although her father wanted her to be a veterinarian, as an adult she chose her own path and became a best-selling toy designer by creating a cuddly pony toy. The toy line now has thirty-five years of development and only minor alterations. My Little Pony has made millions for Hasbro; Zacherle was paid only her Hasbro salary, with a $1 bonus.

DENA BRANNEN

Reston, Virginia

Mountain Dulcimer

This instrument was invented in Appalachia by Scottish and Irish pioneers in the early 1800s. The name "dulcimer" means sweet song, and it is part of the fretted-zither family. The body is made from local wood, such as poplar, walnut, and cherry, and the frets are made from available metal, such as wire used in broom making. It is played on the lap, strummed by a turkey feather or pick, and fretted with a finger or small wooden tool.

STEPHANIE BURKE
Marshall, Virginia

Highland County Maple Festival

Since 1959, the Highland County Maple Festival has celebrated the traditions of making maple syrup with the "opening of the trees." As winter gives way to spring, the sunshine in the lengthening days warms the ground, melting the last of the lingering snow, and the sap begins to rise. Tapping the trees in sugar camps, the residents of Highland County celebrate the rural traditions of generations, cooking down the sap to make maple syrup.

KRISTINE BYRNE
Suffolk, Virginia

The Amazing Peanut

The suitability and popularity of the peanut and peanut products saved the failing farm economy in southeastern Virginia in the aftermath of the Civil War. Peanut farming and processing continue to play a major role in the region's and commonwealth's economy. Brought to the country sometime in the early 1700s by enslaved Africans, peanuts were first grown commercially in this country in Southampton County, Virginia, in the 1840s. The sandy soil of southeastern Virginia was perfect for peanut growing, and the proliferation of peanut farms quickly spread. The development of picking and processing machines and the popularity of peanuts as a snack propelled the lowly legume into a cash crop that saved the Tidewater Virginia farming economy. Dr. George Washington Carver was key to popularizing the peanut. Born into an enslaved family, upon emancipation Carver studied botany and chemistry at Tuskegee University. His treatise on the three hundred uses for peanuts propelled the peanut to star status, and it has become an everlasting fixture of the Tidewater Virginia farming scene.

KATHLEEN DECKER
Williamsburg, Virginia

Historic Eastern State Hospital

The first American hospital devoted exclusively to treating the mentally ill was initially named the Public Hospital of Williamsburg (also known as Eastern State Hospital or Eastern Lunatic Asylum). It was first proposed to the Virginia House of Burgesses by Francis Fauquier in 1766 and admitted its first patient on October 12, 1773. In 1841 the hospital was under the supervision of Dr. John Galt, who introduced "Moral Management" treatment. Dr. Galt opined that mentally ill people "differ from us in degree, but not in kind" and are entitled to human dignity. Dr. Galt introduced therapeutic activities and talk therapy, which were revolutionary treatments at the time. It was ahead of its time in featuring a recovery-based model in the 1800s, including using farming and other occupational skills as treatment. Treatment still focuses on a recovery model today. Current patients are primarily forensic psychiatric patients.

SUSAN DENNING
Herndon, Virginia

Rails to Trails

Rails to Trails is a conservancy that takes no-longer-in-use railroad tracks and turns them into biking, hiking, and walking paths. Nine notable trails cross the Old Dominion through beautiful countryside. Rails to Trails is a brilliant idea that bolsters communities and benefits everyone. The Rails to Trails Conservancy states that these benefits include health and wellness, economic revitalization, transportation options, and improved quality of life. These trails provide riders with an alternative option for travel to work or for pleasure. This can decrease the number of cars on the roads, easing both traffic and pollution. Property values increase near these trails as users develop a proud sense of community, since the trails enhance conservation efforts while providing pleasurable activity.

EILEEN DOUGHTY
Vienna, Virginia

Bringing Back the Chestnut

At one time, the American chestnut tree was a keystone species in the Eastern United States, including much of Virginia and West Virginia. These trees provided food for wildlife; when the nut burrs fell, they were so abundant that they made a sound like thunder in the forest. Many parts of the trees were used by Indigenous peoples and then by European settlers, from house lumber to railroad ties to furniture. From the late 1880s to the 1950s, introduced blights killed the chestnuts in their entire range, completely changing the forest ecology. Memories of presence of the chestnut died out in just a few generations. However, scientists are developing disease-resistant strains, and one important test site is in the State Arboretum of Virginia, near Boyce. Not all tests have been successful, but the future is promising.

EILEEN DOUGHTY
Vienna, Virginia

Power Play

Data centers are being built across the state, both in urban and rural areas. The increase is driven by our insatiable usage of the internet and, even more, by artificial intelligence (AI), which takes an incredible amount of electricity to generate. Neighborhoods are being overwhelmed by the physical presence and noise of these buildings. The power grid struggles to keep up.

KATHY EDWARDS
Alexandria, Virginia

Rt 11 Potato Chips

Rt 11 Potato Chips produced their first batch of old-fashioned kettle-cooked chips in 1992. The company is located on Route 11 in Mount Jackson, Virginia, not far from the Virginia Quilt Museum. Virginia produces many farm products, such as soybeans, peanuts, and cotton, but few people think of Virginia as a place where potatoes are grown. Many of the potatoes used to make the Rt 11 Potato Chips come from a farm near the factory. Their method and high-quality ingredients make an exceptional chip with uncommon character. Visitors to the company can watch potato chips in production during operating hours.

SARAH ENTSMINGER
Ashburn, Virginia

Virginia Lavender

It is believed that lavender was first planted in America shortly after the earliest European settlers arrived in Virginia and made their homes. The plants were brought over as slips (3-to-6-inch branch tips) and as seeds in the holds of the European ships. The plants provided vital food, medicine, and household aids for the early settlers. Recipes for how to use the lavender found their way to colonial America along with the plants. Today, Virginia remains the home of many prosperous lavender farms.

KERRY FARAONE
Purcellville, Virginia

C&O Canal

The Chesapeake and Ohio (C&O) Canal is a historic waterway stretching 184.5 miles along the Potomac River, from Georgetown in Washington, DC, to Cumberland, Maryland. Built between 1828 and 1850, it served as a vital transportation route during the nineteenth century, facilitating the movement of coal, lumber, and agricultural goods from the Allegheny Mountains to eastern markets. For Virginia and West Virginia, the canal was crucial in supporting the region's economic growth, providing an efficient link between rural resources and urban centers. In West Virginia, the canal helped transport coal from nearby mines, fueling industrial and economic development. For Virginia, the canal bolstered agricultural trade and connected communities to broader commerce. Though rendered obsolete by the rise of railroads, the C&O Canal remains an enduring symbol of the region's industrial heritage and is now a cherished national historical park, offering recreation and preserving the history of its contributions to the area's growth.

PRISCILLA B. GODFREY
Philomont, Virginia

Mining in Virginia

In the past, the mining industry was one of the largest employers in Virginia. Mining played a major economic role in Virginia's history. Beginning as far back as 1619 with iron, lead, and zinc mining, throughout the years numerous lucrative minerals were discovered and mined, especially in the Appalachian and Tidewater areas. Coal, gold, iron, copper, pyrite, manganese, and titanium are some of these minerals. Unfortunately, successful mining is often accompanied by subsequent problems with public health, safety, and environmental issues. The Abandoned Mine Land Program came about in the 1970s to address these concerns. With the increase of new roads, bridges, and buildings, the demand for steel and coal has made some mines open up again.

PAULA GOLDEN
Blacksburg, Virginia

Jacket of Plates

This quilt was inspired by jackets (jack) of plates found in Virginia, circa 1610. A jacket of plate was made of small armor plates sewn into a canvas vest, and the plates overlapped to protect against arrows, swords, and other weapons. The jacket of plate was less expensive to produce than custom-made suits of armor and was worn by common soldiers. This type of armor was no longer produced in England around the time of Jamestown's founding. A precursor to today's bulletproof vest, a jack of plate provided the wearer with a greater range of movement and effective protection.

J. E. A. Gibbs

Gibbs used a pocketknife to whittle a crude model of his own version of a sewing machine in 1855. He had seen only the top half of a woodcut version in a newspaper advertisement, but there was little to show him how it actually worked. In the process, he invented his own version, fashioning a flexible looper that required the use of only one thread. After Gibbs's prototype was patented, he collaborated with the father-and-son duo of James and Charles Wilcox.

GLORIA JANE HASSLACHER
Williamsburg, Virginia

Homespun

During the colonial era in Jamestown, settlers tried to cultivate silkworms. Consider the possibility of silk fabric manufactured in the American colonies had the silk-raising experiments succeeded. If colonists had successfully raised silk and woven silk fabric, the fabric would have been considered "homespun." What would have happened if silk, rather than tobacco, had become the important Virginia crop of the day?

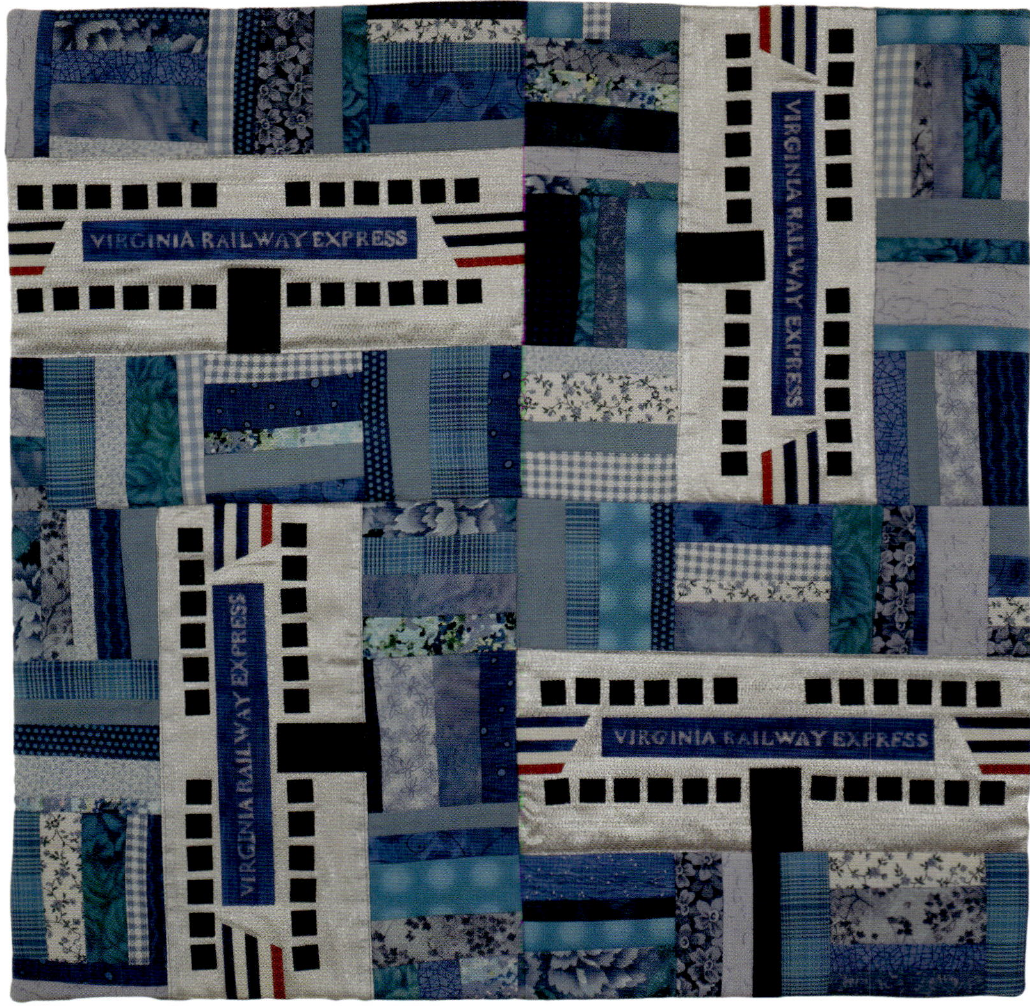

MARJORIE IMGRUND
Sterling, Virginia

Virginia Railway Express (VRE)

The Virginia Railway Express was organized to utilize existing railroads to help bring more workers to DC from the suburbs of Northern Virginia. This commuter train has been used since its first day of service on June 22, 1912. It started with ten stations and sixteen trains that were powered by EMD RP39-2C diesel locomotives. Nowadays, the VRE has nineteen stations and thirty trains, and there are plans for continued growth. Today they use MPI MP36PH-3C locomotives and travel from Union Station in DC toward points west, such as Broad Run / Airport, and south toward Fredericksburg and Spotsylvania County.

BUNNIE JORDAN
Vienna, Virginia

ChapStick

Dr. Charles Browne Fleet was a pharmacist and inventor in the mid-1800s in Lynchburg, Virginia. He developed a formula to prevent and treat dry, chapped lips. Together with his wife, they figured out a clever way to put this formula into what is today a widely recognized tube that twists the product upward for easy application. ChapStick was manufactured in Lynchburg until 1963 and is still made in Richmond. For more than a hundred years, the product has been one of the nation's top choices for lip care. Dr. Fleet was also the inventor of Phospho-Soda, the first personal laxative.

MARY KERR
Woodbridge, Virginia

Cooperative Agriculture

The farming communities in rural Virginia formed the backbone of our eighteenth- and nineteenth-century economies. Experimental processes and cooperative extensions worked hand in hand to promote the research and growth of sustainable Virginia products. Today there are over 39,000 farms operating in our commonwealth, and 95 percent of them are family owned. Agriculture is Virginia's largest private industry and has an economic impact of over $80 billion annually. This quilt was constructed using fragments of a vintage quilt dated circa 1890, a vintage feed sack, vintage tatting, and buttons.

LANA MENGES

Springfield, Virginia

Conservation: Virginia Big-Eared Bat

The appearance of this medium-sized bat is unique because of the relatively large ears and facial glands on either side of the snout. This species risks extinction because of human disturbance and habitat loss. Conservation is an ongoing revolution to protect and preserve our diversity of wildlife in Virginia.

LAURA NELSON

Norfolk, Virginia

Reynolds Wrap

Reynolds Wrap became an American household staple thanks to the Reynolds Metals Company, headquartered in Richmond, Virginia. Aluminum foil was invented in Switzerland in the early 1900s for commercial use. A few years later, it began to be used commercially in the US as wrapping material for candy bars, Lifesavers, and gum. It found its way into American homes when introduced as Reynolds Wrap to American housewives in 1947.

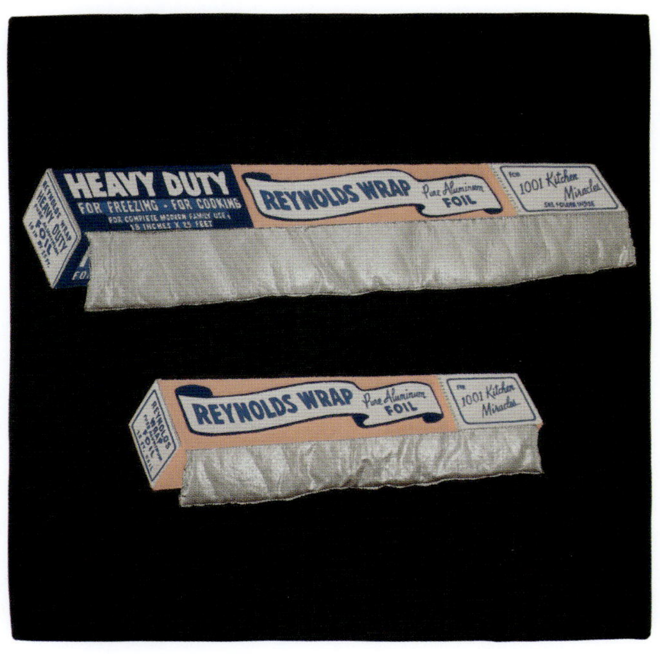

LAURA NELSON

Norfolk, Virginia

Robitussin

Robitussin was created in 1949 by E. Claiborne Robins, a pharmacist. In 1978, over-the-counter Robitussin was touted as the "number one seller among cough preparations in pharmacies," although originally it was sold only to doctors, dentists, hospitals, and pharmacies. The original formulation contained glyceryl guaiacolate and desoxyephedrine hydrochloride, which was blended to form a tasty syrup. With its invention, the company grew into a multibillion-dollar company. The Robins family were large philanthropic donors to the city of Richmond. Their company is now part of Pfizer.

CHERYL PINKERTON

Leonardtown, Maryland

Shenandoah Valley Agricultural Experiment Station

Agricultural experiment stations were first established and funded through the Hatch Act of 1887, to land-grant universities and colleges throughout the US. Virginia Tech hosts one of the oldest continuously operated ram tests (sheep/herd sire evaluation) programs at this location. It is a prime example of disseminating practical knowledge and innovation to benefit US farmers. Since the 1970s the annual Virginia Ram Test has benefited the region's sheep producers and their family farms by offering a source and market of high-quality, performance-tested rams.

CHERYL PINKERTON
Leonardtown, Maryland

The Willcox & Gibbs Chain Stitch Sewing Machine

James Edward Allen Gibbs of Raphine, Virginia, was the clever inventor of this uniquely shaped, cast-iron sewing machine, patented in 1857. Made for home sewing and clothing making, Gibbs's machine features a rotary hook under the cloth plate (instead of a bobbin and bobbin thread). This revolving hook produces a single-thread chain-stitched seam, using only the spool of thread from atop the machine. This was an early labor-saving invention (as was the lockstitch sewing machine) for homemakers. It replaced time-consuming hand sewing to improve the ability to make a whole family's clothing at home.

NANCY ROCHE
Waynesboro, Virginia

Tobacco

In 1612, John Rolfe brought tobacco seeds to the area of Virginia, setting the standard for high-quality plants, and tobacco production spread throughout the region. In 1619 the creation of ports and warehouses to support the sale of tobacco bolstered the development of settlements in Norfolk, Alexandria, and Richmond. By the time of the Revolutionary War, Virginia was said to be the wealthiest colony. Tobacco continued to be an important cash crop in Virginia until the 1990s, when smoking fell out of favor. Today, tobacco is still a significant export of the commonwealth.

CRYSTAL ROUSSEAU
Stafford, Virginia

First Flight

In 1896, Samuel Pierpont Langley, an astronomer, was the secretary of the Smithsonian Institution. He flew an unmanned steam-driven airplane model 0.75 mile for nearly three minutes. This flight took place at Quantico military base. His friend and fellow student Alexander Graham Bell and Frederick Fowle, a photographer at Langley Air Force Base, took pictures of the first flight of the aerodrome. It is now possible to experience flying Langley's drone virtually at Stafford Regional Airport in Stafford, Virginia.

CRYSTAL ROUSSEAU
Stafford, Virginia

Mountain Dew

This soda was originally invented in 1940 in Tennessee and was intended to mix with whiskey. The formula was revised several times, and eventually the rights were obtained by the Tip Corporation of Marion, Virginia. The current version was developed in 1961, and the beverage is now produced and owned by PepsiCo. Mountain Dew sales make up 6.6 percent of soda sales. Residents of Appalachian states such as West Virginia are particularly fond of the drink, and there is even a Mountain Dew Belt, across the states of Kentucky, Ohio, and Minnesota. The urban legend claiming that an ingredient in the soda, Yellow #5, causes a lower sperm count is false. But it is true that Mountain Dew contains more caffeine than other soft drinks.

JANET SAULSBURY
Charlottesville, Virginia

Merrior

In the 1880s, the Chesapeake Bay was producing in excess of 20 million bushels of oysters a year. In 2004 it was estimated that there was only 1 percent remaining of the oyster population. A number of different methods were explored to remediate this oyster crisis. Aquaculture has been proven to help, and the oysters are now raised in special cages. The owners of Rappahannock River Oysters opened a "tasting room" at the oyster farm in Topping, Virginia, in July 2011. Topping is a unique place for raising oysters because it's where the fresh water of the Rappahannock meets the brackish Chesapeake Bay, which is a healthful and mineral-rich environment for them.

MAGGIE WARD
Warrenton, Virginia

The Moon Shines on Franklin County

The making of distilled liquor was both legal and prevalent in Virginia in the late 1800s and early twentieth century. But when Virginia went dry in 1916, followed three years later by the Eighteenth Amendment, the demand for the newly illegal spirits soared. Distillers took to making liquor at night to avoid detection from the federal government; hence the term "moonshiners." According to the Blue Ridge Institute and Museum, ninety-nine out of every one hundred residents in Franklin County were believed to play a part in the moonshine industry in the 1920s. Franklin County is known as "the moonshine capital of the world," and even today illegal moonshine is still made there, with federal raids having occurred as recently as 2001.

BETH WIESNER
Woodbridge, Virginia

Shenandoah Pottery

Pottery production began between 1745 and 1750 in the Shenandoah region and was influenced by German potters from Maryland. The farming community needed pottery products, and that, combined with the availability of earthen and stoneware clays in the valley, enticed tradesmen to the area. The pan in the center of the quilt—designed and made by Solomon Bell of Strasburg—is true to size and would have been used for a variety of purposes, from washing dishes and serving food to letting dough rise and bathing babies. Pottery was essential to the farming community in the 1700s. The establishment of local potters significantly lowered the cost of procuring pottery from the distant cities of Alexandria, Baltimore, and Philadelphia.

KATY WOMACK
Woodstock, Virginia

Virginia Feed Sacks

Feed sacks were born of frugality and became important sources of fabric for home use, especially in impoverished areas of Virginia and West Virginia. Frugal use of feed sacks shows the thriftiness and creativity of the "housewife" in the early years until the 1960s. The Sunbonnet Sue pattern was first introduced in 1870 in England as an illustration on greeting cards. Sue began appearing on our American quilts in the 1930s. Authentic feed sacks were used in the quilt. In the nineteenth century, feed sacks began to replace wooden barrels as a container for dry goods and shipping. They are a perfect example of a utilitarian product turned into something beautiful.

KATY WOMACK
Woodstock, Virginia

Virginia Railroad

The Virginian Railway was conceived in the early twentieth century by William Page and Henry Rogers. Together they built a railroad that transported high-quality "smokeless" bituminous coal from West Virginia coalfields to Hampton Roads, Virginia. The Virginian was built mostly for coal hauling, so it was designed in a straight and steady grade as much as possible. Construction was from 1907 till January 29, 1909, when the last spike was driven near the Virginia and West Virginia line. About 60 percent of the excavation was through solid rock in West Virginia and was done mostly by hand. At the height of the construction, 10,000 laborers were employed. Known for its massive locomotives and 120-ton gondola cars, the Virginian moved the world's longest and heaviest coal trains from Princeton and Deepwater, West Virginia, to Sewell's Point, Norfolk, Virginia, a distance of about 443 miles, where there were loading facilities. The Virginian was in operation from 1909 to 1959, when it was bought by Norfolk and Western Railroad.

CHAPTER 4

We the People

From the everyday to the extraordinary, our quilters have celebrated Virginians. Who is a Virginian? Who got to decide who was a Virginian? We asked our quilters to think beyond the famous people to the local level: Who founded your town? What Indigenous tribes lived in your area before European settlers arrived? How did the enslaved population affect a place? What recent immigrants have helped shape your city? We are honored to present the artists, musicians, writers, scientists, teachers, local politicians, and activists.

Appalachian Folk Dance is a lively quilt that celebrates the people of Virginia and our rich quilting history. This quilt was created in 2004 by members of the Piedmont Quilters Guild of Warrenton, Virginia. Susan Hinkel designed this quilt, preparing kits and supervising its construction. It was hand-quilted by Margie Hockman.

Appalachian Folk Dance Medallion Quilt, Warrenton, Virginia, 98" × 105", 2004. Collection of the Virginia Quilt Museum.

NANCY B. ADAMS
Annandale, Virginia

Rainbow Virginia Reel

The Virginia Reel was a popular folk dance and pastime during colonial times and is still enjoyed today. This is an easy dance, most often engaging a line of four or five couples. It was often saved for the last dance of the night. The traditional Virginia Reel quilt block creates an illusion of curves and movement reminiscent of moves of this barn dance. It is a popular block among quilters because many different effects and results can be achieved with the use of color play.

NANCY B. ADAMS
Annandale, Virginia

JAG Corps Appreciation

The US Army Judge Advocate General's Legal Center and School is located on the campus of the University of Virginia in Charlottesville. Specialized legal education is provided at this exclusive, esteemed, competitive, graduate-level service academy within the US federal government.

NANCY ARICO
Broomall, Pennsylvania

Bojangles

Born in Richmond, Bill "Bojangles" Robinson was an iconic African American tap dancer and actor best known for his Broadway performances and film roles. At the age of six, he started out tap dancing in saloons and grew up in a time when he was able to perform only for Black audiences. Later he performed on Broadway with an all-Black cast for a white audience and eventually was able to join the stage with white actors. He worked regularly as an actor but was best known for his tap-dance routines. He pioneered a new form of tap, shifting from a flat-footed style to a light, swinging method that focused on elegant footwork. He was the highest-paid Black entertainer in the US for the first half of the twentieth century. His life represents the journey of many African American performers.

LISA ARTHAUD
Warrenton, Virginia

Flowing to Freedom

Virginia had the most enslaved persons out of all the states at the beginning of the Civil War. Many are familiar with stories of the South's Underground Railroad slavery escape routes via land. But Virginia had the highest number of enslaved who escaped by water routes. The Chesapeake Bay played a critical role for those escaping slavery.

MARY BETH BELLAH
Charlottesville, Virginia

William & Mary

The College of William & Mary is an iconic institute of higher learning in Virginia. Funded in 1693 under a royal charter issued by King William III and Queen Mary II, it is the second-oldest college in the US. The university offers a multitude of undergraduate majors, minors, and preprofessional programs, and there are myriad areas of study at the graduate and postbaccalaureate level. Centrally located on campus, in a picturesque, wooded area, is the beloved Crim Dell Bridge. Legend has it that if two lovers cross the bridge together and kiss, they will be together for life. The only way to break that spell, if the relationship fails, is for both former lovers to return to the bridge, and the woman must throw the man into the water. It is also said that if someone crosses the bridge alone, they will always be single. A sentimental tradition is the Commencement Walk, when the entire graduating class processes across the Crim Dell together.

SUSAN BLOSS

Front Royal, Virginia

Depth of Sacrifice

On D-Day, June 6, 1944, nineteen soldiers who grew up in Bedford, Virginia, were killed on Omaha Beach in Normandy, France. During the entire invasion, twenty-two Bedford boys were lost, the largest per capita number of soldiers killed from one town on D-Day. The whole town collectively suffered, enabling us to truly appreciate the meaning of sacrificing for our freedoms.

Lord Fairfax, Seventh Lord of Cameron

Lord Fairfax, Thomas Fairfax, originally of Kent, England, was the proprietor of 5.2 million acres of Virginia / West Virginia land, deemed so by Great Britain. As such, he was responsible for enabling many white settlers to establish farms and communities in the Northern Neck of Virginia and in the Shenandoah Valley. His notability is marred by the fact that he was a slave owner.

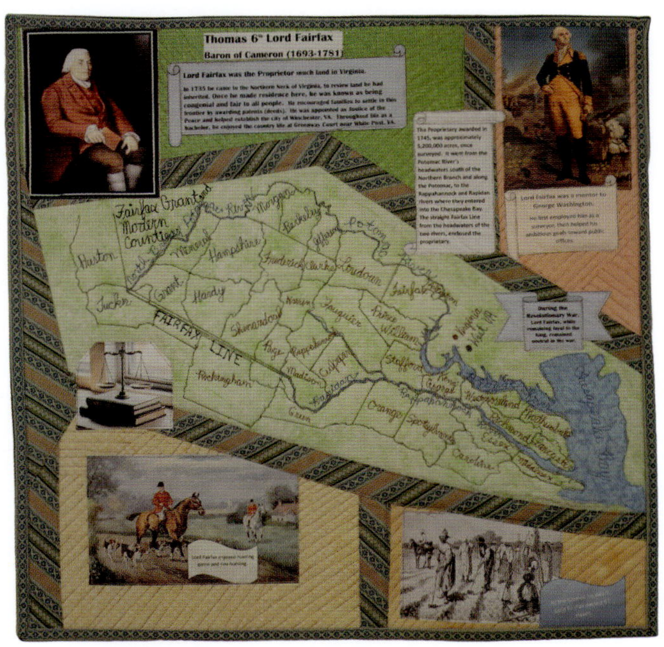

LOIS BORN
Woodstock, Virginia

Virginia Reelin'

The Virginia Reel block brings traditional piecing into this original design. Each Reel block merrily chases itself around in a dance, while the whole is a dance spinning from the greater to the smaller. The visual movement of the block recalls old-time Virginia dancers in their marvelous dresses.

DENA BRANNEN
Reston, Virginia

Pat Sloan

Pat Sloan is a luminary in the Northern Virginia and national quilting scenes. She is a popular and beloved author, fabric designer, developer of quilt patterns, and leader of quilt-alongs. She shares information freely and is an excellent instructor.

DENA BRANNEN
Reston, Virginia

Marvin Audra Lacy

Marvin A. Lacy was a lifelong resident of the Appalachian Mountains community of Summers County, West Virginia. Born in Alderson, West Virginia, he grew up to be a teacher, banker, song leader at church, bowler, fisherman, husband, father, and my grandfather. This portrait is a rendering of his schoolteacher picture from the year my mother was born. He taught in one- and two-room schoolhouses from 1930 to 1945. He was very proud of where he was from and of where he lived, and he instilled the love of southern West Virginia in me.

GLORIA COMSTOCK
McGaheysville, Virginia

Betty Blue Leading the Parade

This pattern celebrating the Fourth of July was illustrated in a 1923 edition of *Woman's World* magazine. It was designed by Ruby Short McKim, who was the editor of the Needlework Department. The traditional English nursery rhyme says, "Little Betty Blue lost her holiday shoe. What shall little Betty do? Give her another, to match the other, and then she'll walk upon two."

GLORIA COMSTOCK
McGaheysville, Virginia

Valley Muse

The Shenandoah Valley was settled by farmer families, many of whom were Mennonite or members of the Church of the Brethren or similar denominations. The valley became the breadbasket for the Revolutionary War and for the Civil War. My ancestor Jacob Loy farmed in Frederick County during the Revolutionary War and paid for a soldier as his substitute, who guarded prisoners in Winchester. Quilting was a necessity, and designs frequently featured pointed motifs, as depicted in the quilt.

BEVERLY AND BILL DASCH
Manassas, Virginia

General and Mrs. George Washington

A Virginian by birth, General Washington was commander in chief of the Continental army during the Revolutionary War and later became the first president of the United States. He served two terms before retiring to his beloved home, Mount Vernon. Martha Washington, also born in Virginia, spent about half of the Revolutionary War near the front lines with her husband. She is considered the nation's first first lady, although this term was not coined until after her death. In his book *Washington: A Life*, Ron Chernow wrote, "George Washington possessed the gift of inspired simplicity, a clarity and purity of vision that never failed him. Whatever petty partisan disputes swirled around him, he kept his eyes fixed on the transcendent goals that motivated his quest."

BEVERLY AND BILL DASCH
Manassas, Virginia

President Thomas Jefferson

Thomas Jefferson was a Virginian who graduated from the College of William & Mary when he was eighteen years of age. In time, he served as the third president of the United States, and he was a statesman, planter, diplomat, lawyer, architect, and philosopher. At just thirty-three years of age, he was the primary author of the Declaration of Independence; 75 percent of his original draft was kept as he wrote it! He is considered one of the most important figures in US history. His memory continues to be honored by the iconic Jefferson Memorial in Washington, DC; on the two-dollar bill and the nickel; and as one-fourth of the Mount Rushmore sculpture in South Dakota.

KATHLEEN P. DECKER
Williamsburg, Virginia

Anne Spencer

Anne Spencer was a famous poet and civil rights activist who lived most of her life in Lynchburg, Virginia. She and her husband, Edward, lived in a house he built from 1901 until her death in 1975. They welcomed writers from the Harlem Renaissance movement into their home, and it served as a cultural salon during the early twentieth century. She was the first African American Virginian to have her poetry anthologized in the prestigious *Norton Anthology* in 1973. She and Edward also started the first NAACP branch in Lynchburg. She was of mixed ethnicity and fought hard for equality both in terms of gender and race.

Ruby Altizer Roberts: Virginia's First Female Poet Laureate

Ruby Roberts (1907–2004) was named Virginia Poet Laureate in 1952, the first female to be so honored. She was a major force in Virginia poetry for decades and edited *The Lyric,* a prominent Virginia poetry journal, from 1952 to 1977. She authored two collections of poetry, three memoirs, a children's book, and a genealogy. She received an honorary doctorate from the College of William & Mary. Roberts mentored many young poets during her lifetime and continues to be an inspiration to female poets.

KATHLEEN P. DECKER
Williamsburg, Virginia

United States Air Force: Aim High—Fly, Fight, Win!

The United States Air Force motto, "Aim High—Fly, Fight, Win!," says it all. The defenders of our airspace have evolved from a tiny balloon force in 1907 within the Department of the US Army Signal Corps to a global force with over 5,500 military aircraft and approximately 400 ICBMs (intercontinental ballistic missiles). As of 2004, it is the world's largest air force, with a $179.7 billion budget and the second-largest service branch of the US armed forces, with 321,848 active-duty airmen, 147,879 civilian personnel, 68,927 reserve airmen, 105,104 Air National Guard airmen, and approximately 65,000 Civil Air Patrol auxiliarists. Thanks to the men and women of our Air Force who patrol the skies, we live free. The Air Force has a prominent presence in Virginia. Langley, located in the Hampton area of the state, was established in 1917 and is said to be one of the oldest continually active air force bases in the world. Virginia is also home to several Air National Guard locations in Richmond, Hampton, Sandston, and Virginia Beach.

DONNA DESOTO
Fairfax, Virginia

Virginia Is for Lovers

Established in 1969, the longest-running tourism slogan in the United States is honored in this piece. The original slogan was Virginia Is for History Lovers, but this was changed to broaden the appeal. In 2009 the beloved saying was inducted into the Madison Avenue Advertising Walk of Fame in New York City. *Advertising Age* called it one of the most successful ad campaigns ever, and *Forbes Magazine* named it one of the top ten tourism-marketing campaigns of all time. Featured on license plates and welcome signs, this slogan has become a well-known and iconic part of American culture. Whatever you love in a vacation, you can find it in Virginia.

ROBERTA DEWEES
Springfield, Virginia

First Recorded Streaker

In 1804 at Washington University in Lexington, Virginia, now known at Washington and Lee University, George William Crump became the first recorded college streaker. Crump ran through the streets of Lexington while wearing only his birthday suit. It is suspected that alcohol and a dare were involved. Crump was arrested for his antics and was suspended for a semester. He continued his studies in New Jersey and Pennsylvania, then went on to serve in the Virginia House of Delegates and the US Congress, and as chargé d'affaires to Chile from 1844 to 1847.

KATHY EDWARDS
Alexandria, Virginia

Dave Matthews Band, "Ants Marching"

The Dave Matthews Band is an American rock band formed in Charlottesville, Virginia, in 1991. Founding members are singer-songwriter and guitarist Dave Matthews, bassist Stefan Lessard, drummer and backing vocalist Carter Beauford, violinist and backing vocalist Boyd Tinsley, and saxophonist LeRoi Moore. As of 2024, Matthews, Lessard, and Beauford are the only founding members remaining in the band; one original member (LeRoi Moore) has passed away, and two other early band members (Peter Greaser and Boyd Tinsley) are still alive but no longer tour with the band. The popular band continues to perform in concerts across the country. The song "Ants Marching" was released in 1995 and is one of their best-known songs.

LISA ELLIS
Harmony, California

Luminescence

Sacred Threads is the name of a unique biennial quilt show that brought many visitors to the Northern Virginia area from 2009 to 2022. This piece, titled *Luminescence,* is a tribute both to the vibrant joy of color and the deep connections we share through quilting. It was created for the "Joy" section of the show by the Sacred Threads committee members, reflecting the spirit that has nurtured this exhibition. The volunteer committee leadership forged deep bonds and lasting friendships as they collaborated to bring the exhibit to life every two years. The show has relocated to Indianapolis and continues its focus on spirituality and inspiration.

KERRY FARAONE
Purcellville, Virginia

Poe

Edgar Allan Poe hunches over his desk, the dim glow of a candle illuminating his pale, intense face. The humid evening air drifts through an open window, carrying the faint scent of the James River and the distant murmur of the city. His quill glides across the paper, each stroke capturing the haunting visions and lyrical despair that define his soul. Around him, the room is sparse; shadowed corners seem to stretch endlessly, as if echoing the gothic depths of his mind. Richmond's vibrant streets lie just beyond, but here, in his solitude, Poe crafts worlds of mystery and melancholy.

LAURA FRASER
Charlottesville, Virginia

Hampton University

In 1861, three enslaved persons fled their owner, a Confederate officer named Col. Charles Mallory, to the Union-held Fort Monroe in Virginia. The Union commander characterized them as "contraband of war" to refuse their return as contemplated under the Fugitive Slave Act, which he said did not apply to secessionists. In 1863, another escapee sat under a large, live oak tree and read the Emancipation Proclamation to others who had sought freedom near Fort Monroe. The tree is now called the "Emancipation Oak." A tower was built in 1868 as part of a chapel to create an institute where African Americans had an opportunity to learn: what is now Hampton University. Even though it took a long time for freed enslaved persons to gain access to equal education in Virginia, the founding of Hampton University was a beginning.

GWEN GOEPEL
Floyd, Virginia

X Marks the Spot

My friend Gibby found six hand-pieced blocks made with fabrics dating to the 1930s in an old trunk in a house that had been moved onto her property. To me, these old blocks represent history and the immigrants who settled into the mountain regions, and they express what could be done with what they had. Fabrics for quilting were often originally from women's skirts and men's shirts and made into items of comfort to keep their family warm. I've rescued these anonymous blocks and used only hand-quilting stitches to honor those who came before me. The importance of Appalachian quilting was to get together and socialize and share daily lives with one another. Our farmhouse in southwestern Virginia still has the holes in one room's ceiling from a quilt frame. This was a common feature: A quilt frame was pulled down from its storage spot as mountain quilters gathered around to stitch their stories together.

SANDI GOLDMAN
Annandale, Virginia

Virginia Star

This piece pays homage to the many Virginia quilters who have influenced me. The block I used was designed by Hazel Carter in 1976. The design also appears in a book by Jinny Beyer published in 2009, titled *The Quilter's Album of Patchwork Patterns*. My interpretation of the block was shaped by the many years of classes I took; I thought it was great that the design was from two well-respected Virginia quilters whom I've had the pleasure of knowing and working with. I like the contemporary feel, and that this was a simple design.

HEIDI HAYNES
Winchester, Virginia

Arthur Ashe—My Hero

Arthur Robert Ashe Jr. was born in Richmond, Virginia, in 1943. He won three Grand Slam singles tennis titles and two in doubles. His top rank was number one in the world in 1968. Ashe was the first African American player selected to the United States Davis Cup team, and the only Black man ever to win the singles titles at Wimbledon, the US Open, and the Australian Open. He helped found the Association of Tennis Professionals (ATP) and the National Junior Tennis League. Arthur Ashe was a legendary tennis professional, educator, and author, and an incredible human being. A civil rights activist who worked for equality in education and philanthropy toward health and opportunities for minority children, he excelled in many endeavors at the height of the civil rights movement in the US. Sculptor Paul DiPasquale, who lives and works in Richmond (and who, incidentally, also made the Neptune sculpture at Virginia Beach), made a bronze statue of Ashe that stands on Monument Avenue in Richmond.

MARJORIE IMGRUND
Sterling, Virginia

Thankful Reflection

So many think of the Pilgrims and Native Americans feasting together as the first Thanksgiving. However, on December 4, 1619, a group of thirty-eight men (including Captain John Woodlief) arrived on the shore of the James River at what is now called Berkeley Plantation. The Virginia Company of London granted them this plantation and several others. One of the expectations from the Virginia Company was that they would give thanks to God for their safe passage. That religious Thanksgiving celebration involved a simple service and most likely fasting instead of feasting. This event was rediscovered 336 years later by Dr. Lyon Tyler. Three years later, in 1958, a new tradition was started at this historic site, called the Virginia Thanksgiving Festival. It has been held every year since.

TONI ISRAEL
Amissville, Virginia

Heaven's on Earth

In 1969, Virginia Tourism promoted the installation of giant-sized LOVE signs, a statewide art project showcasing creativity and warmth that can be found throughout the state. All the signs are singularly designed, but all share the same sentiment: spreading joy and pride of community. Several of these signs are in Culpeper. This quilt is a representation of one of my grandchildren on the Culpeper LOVE sign. I made it to lift up our loved ones and to celebrate the Blue Ridge Mountains being part of the Appalachian Trail. According to the Appalachian Trail Conservancy (ATC), Virginia holds the distinct honor of having the most miles of any state along the trail, at 557 miles.

ANITA PEEPLES JONES
Hyde Park, New York

From Then to Now

Sarah Hulett, enslaved at the Shirley Plantation in Charles City, Virginia, began our family bible, which my husband (Daniel C. Jones) received from his father (Dr. Daniel C. Jones) and has shared with our sons and also our grandson (Isaiah A. Jones). Those who came before led the way for all descendants who follow.

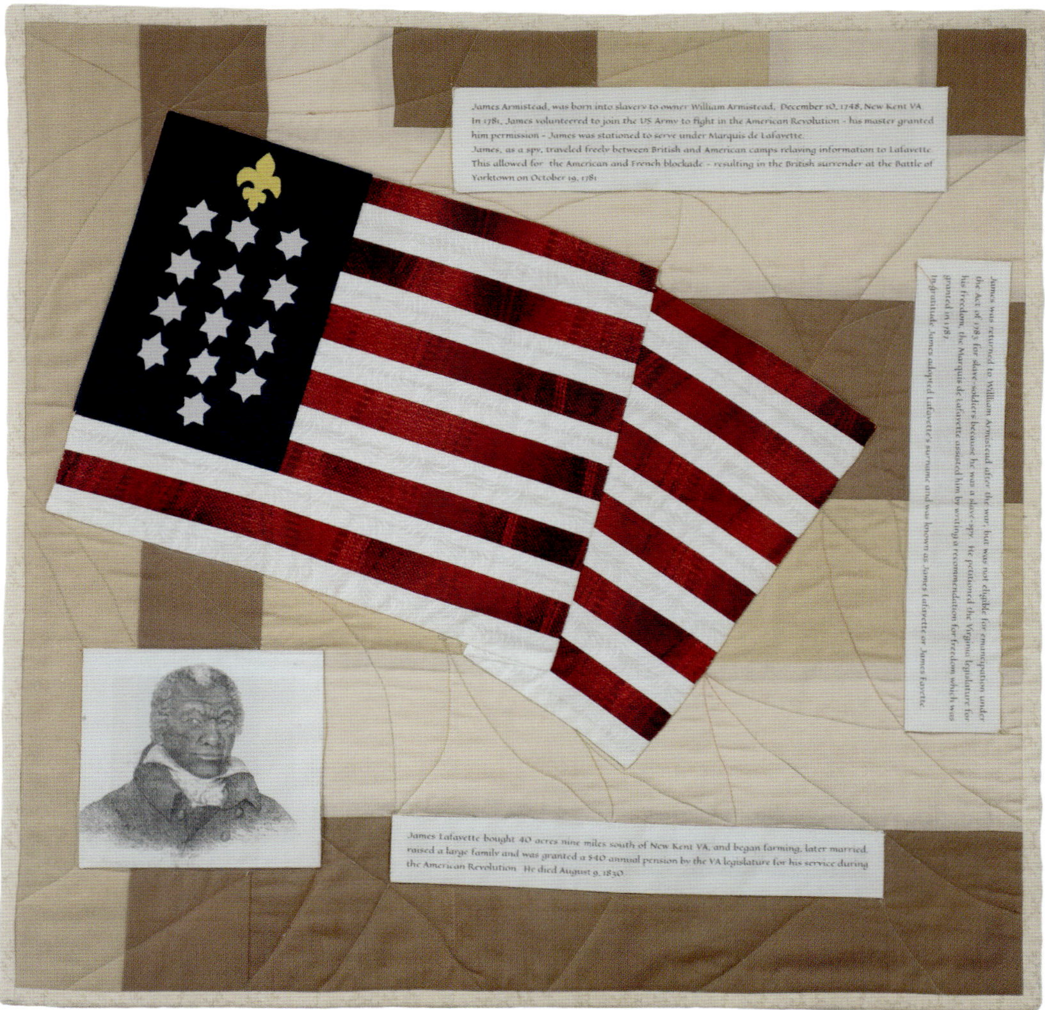

ANITA PEEPLES JONES

Hyde Park, New York

James Armistead and His Role at the Battle of Yorktown

James Armistead was born into slavery and was the "property" of the Armistead family in New Kent, Virginia. When the Revolutionary War came, James was allowed to enlist in the Marquis de Lafayette's regiment. Due to James's detailed knowledge of the roads of Virginia, and his fluency in both French and English, Lafayette realized quickly that James could be best used as a double agent. With James posing as an escaped enslaved person, Lafayette sought out the British, and they freely discussed their war plans in James's presence, as well as considering Benedict Arnold's collaboration with the British. James transmitted details of British plans and spread disinformation to British forces and Benedict Arnold. He is credited for bringing major intelligence to Lafayette that resulted in the defeat of General Cornwallis at Yorktown, and for proving Benedict Arnold was a traitor. After the war, James sought his freedom but his request was denied. However, he was eventually granted 40 acres of farmland and lived out his days as a free man and farmer.

SUSANNE MILLER JONES
Potomac Falls, Virginia

Dr. Sarah Garland Boyd Jones

Sarah Garland Boyd Jones entered Howard University's medical school in 1890, graduated three years later, and was the first African American woman licensed to practice medicine in Richmond, Virginia. Her practice focused on women and children, although all were welcome regardless of race or gender. She and her husband founded Richmond Community Hospital, which was later renamed the Sarah G. Jones Memorial Hospital, Medical College and Training School for Nurses, in her honor.

BUNNIE JORDAN
Vienna, Virginia

Seal of Virginia

The commonwealth of Virginia is known as the Mother of States, the Old Dominion, and the Mother of Presidents. Four of the first five US presidents, and eight in total, were born in Virginia; these presidents include George Washington, Thomas Jefferson, James Madison, James Monroe, William Henry Harrison, John Tyler, Zachary Taylor, and Woodrow Wilson. The state seal of Virginia includes the motto *sic semper tyrannis,* Latin for "Thus always to tyrants." A description of the design, a circle with a sword and the surrounding images, was written by George Wythe and George Mason at the Virginia Convention of 1776.

FRAN KORDEK
Morgantown, West Virginia

Farmer's Fancy

Women often are not recognized for their work. Some are recognized for historically significant contributions, but others are relegated to "women's work," caring for family and home. Despite this, many have demonstrated an unparalleled creative spirit. One example of this creativity is the quilt design Farmer's Fancy. This design was identified in Virginia and West Virginia quilt documentation projects. Both projects reported that these quilts were made in the Shenandoah Valley, an area shared by both states. Most were made in the late 1800s and appeared to have no commercially available pattern, so it was likely a design developed by and shared among quilt makers. It is a challenging design with curved lines and many triangle points. The number of rings varied, with one, two, and three rings documented. It is a design that requires time, patience, and sewing skills. Kudos to the women who made these wonderfully intricate quilts!

KELLY KOUT
Bowie, Maryland

Way to Winchester

The Great Wagon Road was a vital route for trade, communication, and settlement in the eighteenth century. Following long-established Native American trails, it created a route from the port of Philadelphia west to Lancaster, then south into the "backcountry" of Maryland, Virginia, and North Carolina. It allowed local road systems to develop, and it established Winchester as the oldest city in the commonwealth of Virginia, west of the Blue Ridge Mountains.

KIMBERLY MORROW LEONG
Fairfax, Virginia

Satellite

George Mason University began as a satellite campus of the University of Virginia in 1949, and in 1972 it became an independent university. The original buildings on the Fairfax campus are shown here within the outline of the main campus's current area. The three other campuses of George Mason are also outlined and labeled on the surface. Reflecting change as the university grew, regular piecing becomes more staggered, bargello style. This reflects changing norms and expectations. The improv-style piecing reflects growth and changing expectations as George Mason grew to have the largest enrollment for a public university in Virginia. The lines slicing through reflect the turmoil and conflict that comes with growth. The change from dark fabrics to light in the piece reflects a change to the reputation that Mason enjoys today as a nationally recognized research center.

DORA LOCKWOOD
Fairfax Station, Virginia

Pineapple Pizzazz—Old Dominion Hospitality

The pineapple has long symbolized hospitality, with its roots tracing back to the early American colonies. The tradition began when New England sea captains, returning from the Caribbean Islands, brought back exotic fruits and goods from their travels. As a gesture of welcome, these captains would place a pineapple on their fence posts to signal their return and invite neighbors to visit. In a time when sea voyages were long and perilous, this act also symbolized safety and goodwill. Today, the pineapple motif remains a symbol of hospitality, especially in Virginia, where it has evolved into a living tradition. This pineapple quilt block was made as a reminder that the prickly fruit continues to serve as a timeless symbol of the warmth of welcome, the spirit of connection, and the joy of sharing with others.

JANET ACUFF MARNEY
Fairfax, Virginia

My Appalachian Roots

Like most of the people in the Appalachian Mountains of Virginia, my ancestors came across from the British Isles in the early 1700s and thereafter. This piece depicts the traditional heraldic symbols of England, Ireland, Scotland, and Wales, framed by a quatrefoil. The background is faith, representing sea, sky, and mountains. These pioneers endured grueling sea voyages followed by challenging journeys westward to find available land. Many of the skills and character traits brought from the Old World were essential to survival in the beautiful but harsh mountains of the New World. The people were poor but proud, hardworking, stubborn, strong, and independent. They adapted to their new environment in highly creative and competent ways. Their distinctive traits, dialects, Protestant faith, and folk music brought from the British Isles would have great influence on the character, politics, and identity of our emerging nation.

JANET ACUFF MARNEY
Fairfax, Virginia

Quilters Unlimited

Quilters Unlimited (QU) was founded in 1972 to help preserve the tradition, culture, and history of quilting. QU has had a huge influence on quilting in Northern Virginia through excellent programs, workshops, retreats, quilting bees, quilt-ins, annual quilt shows, and displays and demonstrations for the public. In addition, QU members have made thousands of quilts and related items to donate to dozens of charitable organizations. Many warm friendships have been developed over a mutual love of quilts. This tribute piece is deconstructed and adapted from a piece I made for a Quilters Unlimited challenge in 1998.

SANDY MAXFIELD
Raleigh, North Carolina

Dogwood, State Flower of Virginia

The American dogwood (*Cornus florida*) was designated as the state flower in 1918, in part because Thomas Jefferson grew dogwood trees on his Virginia estate, Monticello. Lawmakers saw it as a symbol reflecting the history and heritage of the commonwealth. In 1956, lawmakers doubled down on the dogwood symbol by designating it as the state tree as well, making Virginia the only state to have the same plant as the state flower and state tree. In the spring, the graceful branches of the dogwood tree are loaded with white flowers, which are actually bracts surrounding the small true flowers. To Virginians, the ubiquitous splashes of white, along the edges of woodlands and in gardens everywhere, are the true harbinger of spring.

KATHERINE MCPHERSON
Fairfax Station, Virginia

Alma Mater

James Madison University is nestled in the Shenandoah Valley of Virginia. It was established in 1908 as an all-women's college and became coed in 1966. *Alma mater* in Latin means "nourishing mother," and JMU was a place that nourished my heart and offered an excellent education. Virginia has one of the most highly ranked education systems in the nation. This university has been a part of Virginia and a part of thousands of people's lives for over one hundred years, and it has contributed to the growth and education of many young lives, including mine. Over 75 percent of graduates from JMU are in-state students.

KATHERINE MCPHERSON
Fairfax Station, Virginia

Remembrance

This quilt represents the plane crash into the Pentagon on September 11, 2001. The attack on the Pentagon and on our nation drastically changed the trajectory of the country and impacted millions of Americans. As a child of military personnel living in Virginia, I grew up going to the Pentagon lawn for Fourth of July fireworks, easily entering military installations, and rarely thinking about what my dad's military service might mean. However, after the attack on the Pentagon, the Twin Towers, and the nation, my world, like so many others' around me, was turned upside down. Life as a Virginia military teenager felt surreal; all that I knew changed. We knew people who left to fight in Iraq. When friends talked about joining the military, it took on a whole new meaning; there was a nervous energy that a similar event could happen again, and the joyful ease of being in and out of the Pentagon to visit my dad was gone. Today's current perimeter and security at the Pentagon is a stark reminder of the day it was attacked.

ZOEY MCPHERSON, KATHERINE MCPHERSON, AND MARY KERR
Fairfax Station, Virginia, and Woodbridge, Virginia

January 29, 2025

On January 29, 2025, American Airlines Flight 5342 collided with a Black Hawk helicopter just above Reagan National airport in Washington, DC. Of the sixty-seven people who lost their lives in this tragic accident, twenty-eight were members of the close-knit US figure-skating community. The plane was filled with skaters, coaches, and family members who were returning home from the 2025 Figure Skating National Development Camp in Wichita, Kansas. National Development Camp is an invitation-only, three-day intensive camp for the top-performing juvenile, intermediate, and novice skaters along with their coaches. This camp allows skaters and coaches to have unique training and educational opportunities, and skaters gain exposure to elite programs and Team USA. These athletes are the top performers in their levels and disciplines. The horrible crash affected our entire skating community. This quilt honors the memory of the athletes and members we lost and the community that supported, cherished, and encouraged them.

SUZANNE MEADER
Sterling, Virginia

Waterman Crabbing on Bradford Bay

The photograph that inspired this piece was taken on a trip that Jay Fleming took to Bradford Bay, on Virginia's Eastern Shore, near the town of Wachapreague. This is on a strip of land in southern Virginia between the Chesapeake Bay and the Atlantic Ocean. The seaside town is home to wildlife, workboats, and remote landscapes. Known as the "little city by the sea," it provides rich fishing and crabbing opportunities for locals. A waterman and his helper offer a perfect image of the hardworking men in this region. In their humble watercraft, they are crabbing in the early-morning hours along the peaceful Virginia shoreline.

CAROLE NICHOLAS
Ashburn, Virginia

Stolen Secrets

Antonia Ford was the daughter of a prominent family in Fairfax Court House, now in an area within Fairfax City. Their impressive residence, which still stands today, was a gathering place for Confederate and later Union officers. Antonia charmed them into revealing military secrets, which she passed on to John "Grey Ghost" Mosby and Gen. Jeb Stuart. Her efforts led to the Confederate victory at the Second Battle of Manassas in August 1862 and the subsequent capture of Gen. Edwin Stoughton. Antonia was arrested in 1863 as a spy and imprisoned. Her captor in Washington was Maj. Joseph Clapp Willard, co-owner of the prestigious Willard Hotel, who negotiated her eventual release. After Willard's scandalous divorce, Willard and Antonia were married in 1864. She died in 1871. Antonia represents only one of many female spies who took enormous risks and achieved remarkable results, changing the outcome of battles in the Civil War. Both the Union and Confederacy took advantage of these brave women who, in 1863, the *New York Times* described as "the Delilahs who betray our Samsons."

SUSAN NOVACK
Springfield, Virginia

Rural Virginia: Canning Peaches

The people in this quilt represent country women who came together to do the work of canning the peach harvest on a Virginia farm. They are socializing, having a good time, and sharing in Virginia's bounty as they work. They are intergenerational and multiethnic friends, living their lives framed by the towering beauty of the Peaks of Otter in the Blue Ridge Mountains. This quilt also commemorates the work of celebrated Virginia folk artist Queena Stovall, often referred to as the Grandma Moses of Virginia. Her scenes of everyday country life have delightful details and contain clues to a past, nearly forgotten life in Virginia. Rural women and men in Stovall's paintings can be considered the heart of Virginia. They are not famous, but their principles of neighborliness, inclusion, and hard work laid the foundation of the Virginia where we live today.

JANET R. PALFEY
Fairfax, Virginia

The Waltons

The Waltons was a 1970s television show featuring a retelling of Earl Hamner Jr.'s novel *Spencer's Mountain*. The story was based on Hamner's life during the Great Depression near Schuyler, Virginia, in the Blue Ridge Mountains. The highly popular, family-friendly TV show ran for nine seasons on CBS, portraying a three-generation family who, no matter the trials and tribulations of the day, always wished each other a comforting "Goodnight" at the close of every episode.

CHRISTINE PAYNE
Sterling, Virginia

Pocahontas: A Reflection

We never know what we will be asked to do in our lives. Pocahontas, who lived for only about two decades, has been the source of stories, legends, and film. Although her time on Earth was short, she showed strength and determination in each part of her life. This shows her face as depicted in the Simon van de Passe engraving of 1616, looking at her reflection in a mirror.

CHERYL PINKERTON
Leonardtown, Maryland

Who Tended Virginia's Orchards During WWI?

This quilt honors my paternal grandmother, who patriotically served in the volunteer Women's Land Army of America as a teenager in Leesburg, Virginia. This civilian army was set up in forty states. In Virginia, the orchard fruits harvested by these groups of active, young women contributed to feeding local families during wartime. For this tribute, I pieced a traditional Tree of Life quilt block in colors reminiscent of the WWI era. The patterned fabric under the tree showcases wheelbarrows, pruning shears, watering cans, and other orchard-tending tools. This was a necessary and emerging role for young women to help support the country's agricultural needs.

SUSAN PRICE

Springfield, Virginia

Defenders of Democracy

Three generations of the Hopkins family (my husband's family) served in the military in four different wars. They are an African American family with roots in Franklin County, Virginia, who went on to serve in other ways after their military service. Without these brave Defenders of Democracy, where would we be? We need the sacrifices of ordinary people who answer the call to defend our country.

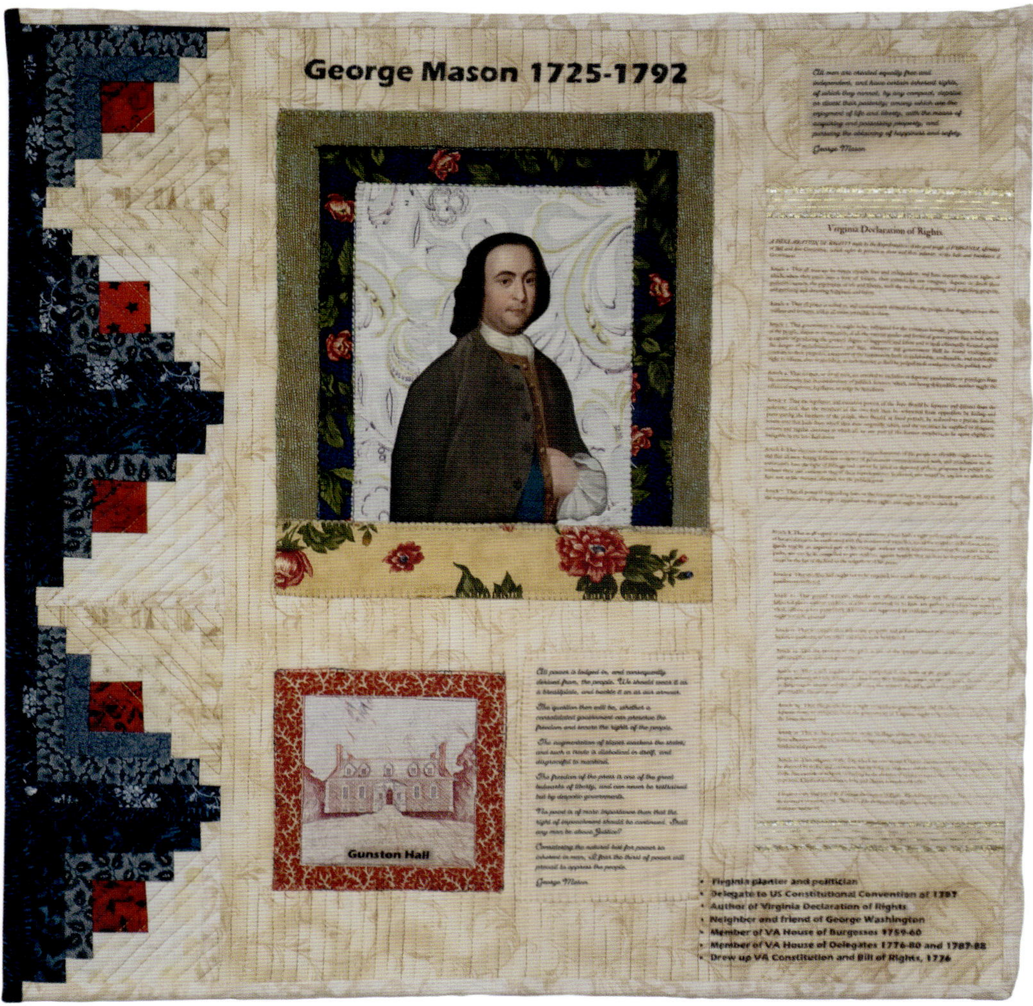

SUSAN PRICE
Springfield, Virginia

George Mason

George Mason IV, planter and politician, was the fourth generation of his family in America. His family owned thousands of acres along the Potomac River in both Maryland and Virginia. He was well educated by tutors and relatives and took his place as an influential member of the community. After marrying Ann Eilbeck in 1750, they moved to the property that became home to Gunston Hall. They had twelve children, nine of whom lived to adulthood. Ann died in childbirth at age thirty-nine. A strong advocate of individual rights, he is best known as the author of the Virginia Declaration of Rights, which became the basis for the US Bill of Rights. He was a delegate to the Constitutional Convention of 1787 but did not sign the Constitution due to its lack of a bill of rights. He was a member of the Virginia House of Burgesses and later the Virginia House of Delegates. In 1776 he drafted the Virginia Constitution and the Bill of Rights. Along with James Madison, he wrote the presidential oath of office. In 1791 the federal Bill of Rights was ratified and became the law of the land. George Mason died in 1792 at age sixty-seven.

JULIE RIGGLES
Annandale, Virginia

Quilting in the Style of Jinny Beyer

The prestigious Jinny Beyer Studio was located in Great Falls, Virginia. Jinny's border print designs were unique; no one else has designed mirror-image border prints that are both versatile and beautiful. Jinny has authored several books, has traveled all over the world teaching, and has always been a traditional quilter with a design flair like no other. She is a gem in our quilting world. Jinny Beyer fabric was used exclusively in this quilt.

JANET SAULSBURY
Charlottesville, Virginia

Honky Tonk Angel

Born in Winchester in 1932 and killed in a plane crash in 1983, Patsy Cline was the first woman elected to the Country Music Hall of Fame, in 1973. She is known as one of the first women to sell records and headline concerts, and is one of the first country music artists to cross over into pop music. Fans can visit her childhood home in Winchester, which is now a museum.

PRISCILLA STULTZ
Williamsburg, Virginia

Governor Doug Wilder

Lawrence Douglas Wilder is a lawyer and politician who served as the governor of Virginia from 1990 to 1994. He was the first African American ever elected to serve as governor of a US state. The US is slowly becoming more inclusive, with greater numbers of politicians, educators, healthcare workers, and other influencers of color. We are grateful for trail blazers like Doug Wilder.

KATHRYN CRUMP TEAGUE
Burke, Virginia

Missy, Missy

Missy Elliot's Virginia roots run deep, and her contributions to her community and influence in the music world are prolific. She is the winner of numerous BET Hip Hop awards, MTV Music Video awards, and multiple Grammys. All this and more led to Portsmouth, Virginia, renaming a street in her honor and the governor of Virginia declaring October 17 as "Missy Elliot Day." In 2022 she was awarded the National Medal of Arts by the president of the United States and is in both the Songwriters Hall of Fame and the Rock and Roll Hall of Fame. That makes her a "monumental mother."

KARLA VERNON
Vienna, Virginia

The First Virginians

This illustrates the Native American Tribes throughout the state, circa 1600s, organized by language groups. The border contains the symbols of tribes recognized by the commonwealth of Virginia. It is important to know who the First Virginians were, and many do not know which tribes lived here before the English settlers arrived. The background of the quilt is a Virginia Beauty block. The map of Virginia also shows the "Great Warriors' Path" and trade routes.

ARLENE WAGNER
Falls Church, Virginia

Whimsical George

It is important to commemorate George Washington because he is known as one of the founding fathers of our country, particularly for his role in bringing about American independence from England in the Revolutionary War. He served two terms as the first president of the US. He inherited his Mount Vernon plantation estate from his half brother. The site is now among the most-sought-after tours for visitors to the Washington, DC, area. A cherry tree in included in this whimsical piece because, although the chopping down of the cherry tree and the statement "I cannot tell a lie" are fabrications, these are part of our American folklore.

MIRANDA WALKER
Rockingham, Virginia

Booker T. Washington

Booker T. Washington was born in Franklin County, Virginia, on April 5, 1856, and played a significant role in the commonwealth's history. Washington was born into slavery, and his early life shaped his future endeavors and philosophies. After the Civil War, Washington moved to Malden, West Virginia, where he worked in salt furnaces and coal mines while pursuing his education. He eventually graduated from what is now Hampton University in 1875. He is best known as the first headmaster of the Tuskegee Normal and Industrial Institute (now Tuskegee University) in Alabama. He strongly believed in practical, vocational training as a means for African Americans to achieve economic self-reliance and social progress. Washington's legacy is also commemorated at the Booker T. Washington National Monument in Hardy, Virginia.

MIRANDA WALKER
Rockingham, Virginia

Ella Fitzgerald

Born in Newport News in 1917, Ella Fitzgerald became one of the most influential jazz vocalists of all time. Known as the "First Lady of Song," she possessed an unmatched vocal range. Despite early hardships, including the loss of her mother and time spent in a reform school, her talent and determination led her to stardom. Her breakthrough came in 1934, when she won an amateur contest at the Apollo Theater, launching a career that spanned six decades. Beyond her music, she quietly broke racial barriers, challenging segregation by refusing to perform for segregated audiences and securing opportunities for Black artists. She recorded over two hundred albums, won thirteen Grammy Awards, and became a global icon. Her contributions to music and civil rights continue to inspire, and her legacy is honored in Virginia through institutions such as the Ella Fitzgerald Theater in Newport News.

MIRANDA WALKER
Rockingham, Virginia

Made by the Band

Pharrell Williams, born in Virginia Beach in 1973, is a visionary artist, producer, and entrepreneur whose influence spans music, fashion, and philanthropy. His musical journey began with his high school marching band, the Princess Anne's Fabulous Marching Cavaliers. He played the snare drum, a role he credits for shaping his career. Rising to fame as part of The Neptunes, Williams has produced or coproduced hundreds of tracks for a wide array of artists. He is also a fashion icon, and wearing oversized hats became Williams's signature look. A champion for education and social change, he has launched initiatives such as YELLOW, a nonprofit dedicated to empowering youth through music, education, impeccable phrasing, and a signature scat-singing style.

KEVIN WOMACK
Forest, Virginia

Scribbles for Cy

Cy Twombly, an American painter, sculptor, and photographer (1928–2011), was a native of Lexington, Virginia. He utilized a gestural style of painting to create large-format, graffiti-like work. His paintings, while appearing deceptively simple and childlike, took days or weeks of contemplation and planning before completion. Twombly brings emotion and storytelling to an abstract style. As a fellow mark maker, I work similarly to this artist, striving to import emotion and meaning into the cloth as I print and layer imagery. Cy Twombly often used scribbles in his work. As a fellow Virginian who loves abstract expressionism, I feel a kinship to Cy. Honoring him and his work was a natural choice for me.

About the Virginia Quilt Museum

Photo: Eileen Matsumura, Layton, Utah

Whether you're a seasoned quilter or simply someone who appreciates the artistry and history of quilts, the Virginia Quilt Museum offers a unique and enriching experience that celebrates the enduring legacy of this beloved craft. In 1995, the Virginia Quilt Museum opened with a collection of just fifteen quilts and the determination and support of individuals and guilds throughout Virginia. There was a desire to share Virginia's rich quilt-making history, which had been passed down through generations.

In the 1980s, the Virginia Consortium of Quilters, a nonprofit statewide organization, initiated the project of documenting quilts in Virginia to preserve the stories, pictures, and information for historical research. Joan Knight, a leader of the documentation project, promoted the idea of a museum in the early 1990s. In support of this effort, the Virginia Consortium of Quilters provided the seed money for a museum. Joan Knight was the museum's first director when the doors opened in the historic Warren-Sipe House in downtown Harrisonburg, Virginia, in 1995. Within ten years, the museum's collection had increased tenfold to over 150 quilts. In 2000 the Virginia General Assembly passed a resolution designating the museum as the Official Quilt Museum of the Commonwealth.

The year 2024 marked another exciting milestone, when the museum relocated to the historic Silver Lake Mill in Dayton, Virginia. This beneficial move provided a more spacious setting for exhibits and a larger workspace, as well as greater accessibility and comfort for visitors. Quilt exhibits and quilts in the collection have featured every style of quilting, including historical, traditional, modern, and contemporary art, showing the diversity and evolution of quilting. The permanent collection has expanded to over three hundred quilts, dating from the early 1800s to present day. A separate collection is designated as educational, allowing the museum to take quilts into the community to share and teach. There is also a sewing-machine collection, including machines significant to Virginia history or the history of sewing machines.

The Virginia Quilt Museum plays a crucial role in preserving, interpreting, and promoting the art of quilting. By fostering education, appreciation, and recognition for quilting, the museum has made invaluable contributions to the quilting community and continues to be an important cultural institution as Virginia quilters continue Stitching Together History.

Bunnie Jordan
Quilt historian and former Virginia Quilt Museum board member

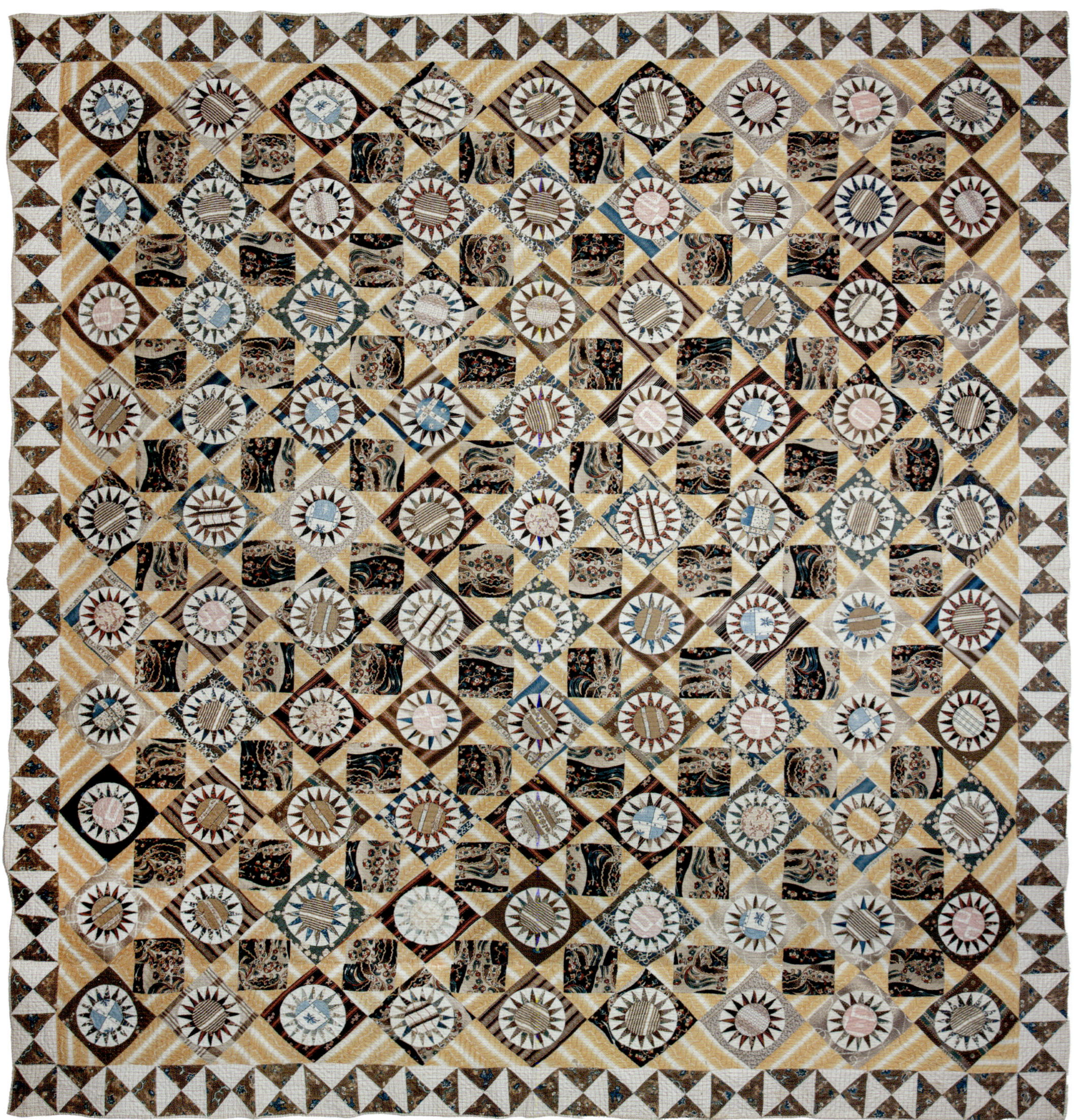

Acknowledgments

Thank you to the generous community of quilters who shared their unique talent, time, and passion to make this project a reality. Their work and words truly reflect the many facets of our rich Virginia history. Thank you to Alicia Thomas, executive director of the Virginia Quilt Museum, whose vision and organization orchestrated this enormous undertaking to collect and exhibit 250 quilts. In fact, more than 250 quilts resulted from the call to artists! All of the quilts, including the overflow, will be shown at the museum. Thank you to the Board of Directors at the museum, who wholly supported this multiyear endeavor.

Thank you to Katherine McPherson for her excellent photography skills and also to Bunnie Jordan for her foreword, historical information, and encouragement.

We are grateful to our editor, Sandra Korinchak, and the staff at Schiffer Publishing, Ltd., for their unending encouragement, patience, and support.

All proceeds from this project go to the Virginia Quilt Museum as they continue their mission of cultivating and preserving the quilting arts in Virginia.

It has been our honor to work with this army of quilt enthusiasts.

Sunburst Quilt, unknown maker, Virginia, 90" × 95.5", circa 1830. Collection of the Virginia Quilt Museum.

Mary Kerr is an American Quilt Society–certified appraiser, quilt curator, and award-winning quilter. She has been a quilt instructor for more than forty years, and her current lectures and workshops focus on quilt history and the preservation of antique textiles. She is the author of many books on quilting, including *Southern Quilts*. marykerr.com

Donna Marcinkowski DeSoto is a fiber artist, art quilt curator, and the author of several quilt books, including *Inspired by the Nation's Capital*. She has resided in Virginia for more than forty years, quilting all the while. inspiredquilts.com

The Virginia Quilt Museum cultivates and preserves the quilting arts in Virginia. Nestled in the heart of the picturesque Shenandoah Valley, the museum promotes quilting's unique blend of art and cultural heritage. vaquiltmuseum.org